John D. M. Williams.

INSTITUTES

OF

NATURAL and REVEALED

RELIGION.

VOL. I.

CONTAINING

The Elements of NATURAL RELIGION ;

To which is prefixed,

An Effay on the beft Method of communicating religious Knowledge to the Members of Chriftian Societies.

By JOSEPH PRIESTLEY, LL. D. F.R.S.

Wifdom is the principal Thing.

SOLOMON.

LONDON:

Printed for J. JOHNSON, No. 72, in St. Paul's Church-Yard, MDCCLXXII.

Another one

3 v

Mrs. g. D. W. Williams

337,782

Nov. 13, 1883

To the younger part of the
congregation of Protes-
tant Dissenters at Mill-
Hill, in Leeds.

My young friends,

IT was on your account that I com-
posed these *Institutes of natural
and revealed religion*, and to you I
take the liberty to dedicate them.

It is the earnest wish of my heart,
that your minds may be well esta-
blished in the found principles of
religious knowledge, because I am fully persuaded, that nothing else can
be a sufficient foundation of a virtuous and truly respectable conduct in
life, or of good hope in death. A

mind

mind deftitute of knowledge (and, comparatively fpeaking, no kind of knowledge, befides that of *religion,* deferves the name) is like a field on which no culture has been beftowed, which, the richer it is, the ranker weeds it will produce.   If nothing good be fown in it, it will be occu- pied by plants that are ufelefs or noxious.

Thus the mind of man can never be wholly barren.   Through our whole lives we are fubject to fuccef- five impreffions; for, either new ideas are continually flowing in, or traces of the old ones are marked deeper. If therefore, you be not acquiring good principles, be affured that you are acquiring bad ones ; if you be not forming virtuous habits, you are, how infenfibly foever to your felves, forming vicious ones ; and, inftead

of

of becoming thofe amiable objects in yourfelves, and thofe valuable members of fociety, which nature, and the God of nature intended that you fhould be, you will be at beft, ufelefs *cumberers of the ground*, a dead weight upon the community, receiving fupport and advantage; but contributing nothing in return; or you will be the pefts of fociety, growing continually more corrupt yourfelves, and contributing to the corruption of others.

Finding yourfelves, therefore, in fuch a world as this, in which nothing is at a ftand, it behoves you ferioufly to reflect upon your fituation and profpects. Form, then, the generous refolution (and every thing depends upon your refolution) of being at prefent what you will certainly wifh you had been fome years hence, what your beſt friends wiſh you to be, and what your maker has intended, fitted, and enabled you to be.

Above all things, be careful to improve and make uſe of the *reaſon* which God has given you, to be the guide of your lives, to check the extravagance of your paſſions, and to aſſiſt you in acquiring that *knowledge*, without which your rational powers will be of no advantage to you. If you would diſtinguiſh yourſelves as *men*, and attain the true dignity, and proper happineſs of your natures, it muſt be by the exerciſe of thoſe faculties which are peculiar to you as men. If you have no higher object than the gratification of your animal appetites and paſſions, you rank yourſelves with the *brute beaſts* ; but, as you will ſtill retain that *reflection*, which

which they have not, you will never
have that unallayed enjoyment of a
senfual life which they have. In
fact, you are incapable of the happinefs of brute animals. Afpire,
therefore, to thofe fuperior purfuits,
and gratifications for which you were
formed, and which are the preroga-
tive and glory of your natures.

Let me urge you, my younger
hearers, to a more than ordinary attention to regularity and propriety of
behaviour, becoming men and chriftians, that your conduct may be no
difgrace to the *rational and liberal fen-*
timents, which I truft you have im-
bibed. Let it be feen, that when
God is confidered as the proper object of reverence, love, and confidence, as the benevolent Father of
all his offspring of mankind, and their
righteous and impartial moral gover-

nor,

nor, the principle of obedience is the moft ingenuous and effectual. Cherifh the moft unfeigned gratitude to the *Father of lights,* that your minds are no longer bewildered with the gloom and darknefs, in which our excellent religion was, for fo many ages, involved; but let this confideration be a motive with you to walk as becomes fo glorious a light. If your conduct be fuch as, inftead of recommending your own generous principles, furnifhes an excufe to others, for acquiefcing in their prejudices and errors, all the difhonour which is thereby thrown upon God, and the injury which will be done to the pure religion of Jefus Chrift, by keeping it longer in a corrupted ftate at home, and preventing its propagation abroad, will be your peculiar guilt, and greatly aggravate your condemnation.

Value

Value the *scriptures*, as a treasury of divine knowledge, consisting of books which are eminently calculated to inspire you with just sentiments, and prompt you to right conduct; and consider them also as the only proper *authority in matters of faith.*

In a thing so interesting to you as the business of *religion*, affecting the regulation of your conduct here, so as to prepare you for immortal happiness hereafter, respect no *human authority* whatever. Submit to those who are invested with the supreme power in your country, as your lawful *civil magistrates*; but if they would prescribe to you in *matters of faith*, say that you have but one *Father even God*, and *one Master even Christ*, and *stand fast in the liberty with which he has made you free.* Respect a *parliamentary king*, and chearfully pay all

parliamentary

parliamentary taxes; but (with a re-
fpectable member of the Britifh houfe
of Commons, in the debate relating to
the act of William and Mary, which
makes it confifcation of goods and
imprifonment for life, to deny the
doctrine of the Trinity) have nothing to do with a *parliamentary religion,* or a *parliamentary God.*

Religious rights, and *religious liberty,* are things of ineftimable value.
For thefe have many of our anceftors
fuffered and died; and fhall we, in
the funfhine of profperity, defert that
glorious caufe, from which no ftorms
of adverfity or perfecution could make
them fwerve. Let us confider it as a
duty of the firft rank with refpect to
moral obligation, to tranfmit to our
pofterity, and to provide, as far as we
can, for tranfmitting, unimpaired, to
the lateft generations, that generous
zeal

zeal for religion and liberty, which makes the memory of our forefa- thers fo truly illuftrious.

So long as it fhall pleafe that God, in whofe hands our breath is, and whofe are all our ways, to continue me in that relation, in which I think my- felf happy in ftanding to you at pre- fent, I truft that I fhall not fail to endeavour to imprefs your minds with a juft fenfe of what you owe to God, to your country, and to mankind. Let it be our mutual care to derive the moft durable advantage from our prefent temporary connection, by growing continually more *eftablifh- ed, ftrengthened, and fettled,* in the habit and practice of all the virtues which become us as men and as chriftians; that we may fecure a hap- py meeting, and mutual congratula-

       tion

tion in the future kingdom of our Lord and Saviour.

I am,

My young friends,

with affection and efteem,

your brother, and fervant,

in the gofpel of Jefus Chrift,

JOSEPH PRIESTLEY.

Leeds, March, 1772.

THE PREFACE.

NO branch of knowledge can be taught to advantage except in a regular, or syftematical method. It is also very convenient, both for the teacher and the learner, to have the *elements* of any science drawn up in a fuccinct manner; by the help of which the one may be directed in what order to explain the several branches of it, and the other may fee at one view all its conftituent parts, in their natural connection, and thereby gain the moft comprehenfive and diftinct idea of the whole, which is also a great advantage for retaining it in memory.

It was with a view to the inftruction of youth that the following *Inftitutes* were compofed, and nothing more was meant, originally, than to furnifh myfelf with an eafy method of difcourfing upon the fubjects of natural and revealed religion to the

young.

young men of my own congregation, whom I formed into a clafs for that purpofe. But when I was induced to publifh them, for the benefit of others, I made them a little fuller, that thofe young perfons who can have little or no affiftance in their inquiries, might be able to read them with tolerable advantage. I fhall think myfelf happy if this *manual* be the means of eftablifhing any of the youth of the prefent age in the found knowledge of thofe moft important fubjects to which it is appropriated. I am fatisfied that no man can write, or live, to better purpofe.

As my fole view in this fhort fyftem was to teach the elements of religious knowledge to perfons intended for *common and civil life,* and not for any of the learned profeffions, I have avoided, as much as I poffibly could, thofe metaphyfical and abftrufe fpeculations, which have been raifed from every branch of my fubject, and have chiefly confined myfelf to fuch confiderations as are moft adapted to produce conviction in the minds of

thofe

thofe who are not much ufed to clofe reflection ; and I have endeavoured through
the whole to exprefs myfelf with the greateft clearnefs and precifion. For this purpofe I have been obliged to depart confi-
derably from the plan of any treatife that
I have yet feen upon thefe fubjects.

I am far, however, from being able to
promife that I fhall leave thefe fubjects
free from all obfcurity. The mind of
man will never be able to contemplate the
being, perfections, and providence of God
without meeting with inexplicable difficulties. We may find fufficient reafon for
acquiefcing in the darknefs which involves
thefe great fubjects, but we muft never
expect to fee them fet in a perfectly clear
light. But notwithftanding this, we may
know enough of the divine being, and of
his moral government to make us much
better and happier beings than we could
be without fuch knowledge ; and even
the confideration of the infuperable difficulties referred to above is not without its
ufe, as it tends to imprefs the mind
                                    with

with sentiments of reverence, humility, and submiffion.

I have also had another view in not chufing to conceal fome of the great difficulties which attend the demonftration, if not of the *being*, yet of the moft effential *attributes*, and moral *government* of God. It was that the confideration of them might make us more fenfible of the value of *revelation*, by which many of them are, in a great meafure, cleared up, and by which great light has been thrown upon every important branch of natural religion.

Many unbelievers avail themfelves very much of the *diverfity of opinions* which prevails among the profeffors of revealed religion, and boaft of the great *clearnefs*, as well as *fufficiency of the light of nature* ; but the cafe is much otherwife; and there have been, in fact, among men of the greateft learning and acutenefs of thought, believers and unbelievers in revelation, as great a diverfity of opinion with refpect to the principles of natural, as of revealed religion ;;

religion; and notwithstanding the various sentiments of christians, they are all
perfectly agreed, and unanimous, with
respect to all the most important doctrines
of natural religion, concerning which unbelievers in revelation have never been
able to arrive at any certainty, or uniformity of opinion; so that men who
think at all are very far from getting rid
of any real difficulty by abandoning revelation. Nay the difficulties which we shall
find upon this subject among christians,
though I shall not fail to state them with
the greatest fairness, suppressing nothing
that can contribute to their strength, are
by no means so embarrassing to the mind
of man, as those which occur in the contemplation of nature.

If any person, discouraged by these
difficulties, should think to relieve himself by rejecting *all religion*, natural and
revealed, he will find, if he reflect at all,
that he has miserably deceived himself,
and that he is involved in greater perplex-
ity than ever; the scheme he has adopted

not

not only filling his mind with great darknefs and diftrefs, but being contrary to
fome of the plaineft appearances in nature, and therefore manifeftly irrational
and abfurd. In this cafe, therefore, true
philofophy will lead a man to acquiefce
in that fcheme of principles which is attended with the feweft difficulties, without
expecting to meet with any that is quite
free from them; and a good man will
be drawn by a ftrong propenfity to em-
brace that fyftem, the contemplation and
influence of which will tend to make him,
and his brethren of mankind, moft virtuous and happy. This important circumftance will always operate as an evidence for the truth of natural and revealed
religion, on minds which are not pervert-
ed by fophiftry, or vice.

In the fecond and third parts of thefe Inftitutes, which relate to the duty and final
expectations of mankind, it will be feen that
I have made great ufe of *Dr. Hartley's obfervations on man.* To this writer I think
myfelf happy in having any fair opportunity of making my acknowledgements,

and

and I fhall think that a very valuable end
will be gained, if, by this or any other
means, a greater degree of attention
could be drawn upon that moft excellent
performance, fo as to make it more generally read, and ftudied, by thofe who are
qualified to do it. I do not know any
thing that is better adapted to make an
impreffion upon truly philofophical minds
than the fketch that he has given of the
evidences of chriftianity, in his fecond vo-
lume; and for this reafon I fhould be exceedingly glad to fee that part of his
work publifhed feparately.

An

AN ESSAY ON THE BEST METHOD OF COM-
MUNICATING RELIGIOUS KNOWLEDGE
TO THE MEMBERS OF CHRISTIAN SO-
CIETIES.

THE fuperficial knowledge, or rather the extreme ignorance of the
generality of youth in the prefent age,
with refpect to religion, is the fubject of
great and juft complaint; and for want of
being well eftablifhed in the principles of
rational religion, many of them are daily
falling a prey to *enthufiafm* on one hand,
and *infidelity* on the other. In this life
we muft not expect any good without fome
attendant evil. The circumftance of
which we now complain has been, in part,
the natural effect of the moderation of the
prefent times, in which no perfon is even
queftioned about his religion. For as the
fubject is never canvaffed, nor fo much as
ftarted in polite company, no perfon thinks

it

it worth his while to prepare himfelf for making any reply, and confequently the youth of this age never profeffedly ftudy the fubject, or ever give more than an occafional and curfory attention to it.

Another fource of this complaint is the little care that is now taken by parents in the religious inftruction of their children. They condemn the feverity with which they recollect that they themfelves were treated, and, not confidering the advantage which they derive from it, exclaim againft fuch exceffive rigour and aufterity, and throw off not only the *tutor*, but almoft the *mafter* too with refpect to their children; not recollecting that, after this, there is little left of the *parent* that is tru'r valuable. To this conduct they are, no doubt, at the fame time, fecretly influenced by a regard to their own eafe; for upon the prefent fafhionable plan, a perfon gives himfelf very little trouble indeed about forming the minds of his offspring; and fome may think that they have fufficiently done their duty in this refpect, when

when they have provided them with *mafters,* to fuperintend their education in general.

Many perfons will not readily adopt my fentiments relating to this fubject. For my own part, however, I have not the leaft doubt, but that, though the maxims of our forefathers may have been too ftrict, we of the prefent age are already far gone in another extreme, oppofite to theirs, and much more dangerous. Their method, by reftraining the inclinations of youth, might (though, perhaps, upon the whole, it might not) diminifh the happinefs of that early period of life ; and in fome inftances, I doubt not, the exceffive reftraints they were under might ferve to inflame their paffions, and prepare them for the more unbounded and criminal indulgence of them, when they became their own mafters ; but, in general, habits of fobriety and moderation were, by this means, effectually formed, and a difpofition to licentioufnefs intirely precluded.

On

On the contrary, our greater indulgence to youth gives them more *liberty*,
but, perhaps, not more real *enjoyment* even
of early life; but whatever good effect
this conduct may have upon fome ingenuous tempers, I am fatisfied that, in general, it is fatal to virtue and happinefs.
through life. Our youth having had little or no reftraint put upon their inclinations, and religious principles not having
been fufficiently inculcated, they give the
reins to pleafure, at that critical time of
life, in which the paffions are peculiarly
ftrong, and reafon weak; and the authority of a parent not interpofing, where it
is moft wanted, a difpofition to licentioufnefs is compleatly formed, and fuch bad
habits are contracted, as too often end in
utter profligacy and ruin. At beft, their
minds not having been feafoned with the
principles of religion, they become mere
men of the world, without vice, perhaps,
but alfo without virtue.

Alfo, in confequence of the fame fuperficial education, to fay the leaft of it,
our

our youth having never thought upon the fubject of religion, inftead of entertaining thofe enlarged fentiments of *religious liberty*, which will never be wholly extinct in the breafts of their parents, the flighteft inducement is often fufficient to make them abandon the *diffenting intereft*, the value of which they were never taught to underftand; and to make them conform to the eftablifhed religion of this, and, for the fame reafon, to that of any other country in the world, attended with fufficient temporal encouragement.

With the difufe of *family prayer*, the regular *reading of the fcriptures* has alfo been laid afide; fo that in moft of our opulent families, the youth have hardly an opportunity of making themfelves acquainted with the contents of thofe books which are the fource of all religious knowledge. When the bible, if there be one in the family, is wholly neglected by the parent, what inducement can the fon have to look into it ?

A falfe

A falfe tafte, and a pretended reverence for the fcriptures has, likewife, ba-
nifhed them from many of our fchools ;
fo that, except their being read in detach-
ed and unconnected portions, in places of
public worfhip, many perfons, it is to be
feared, would live and die in the utter
ignorance of the contents of their bibles.

With this neglect of family difcipline,
the neglect of difcipline in our churches,
which has been owing to fimilar caufes,
has likewife concurred. In many of our
focieties, the bufinefs of *catechifing* has,
likewife, been laid afide, nor has any thing
been fubftituted in its place, as better a-
dapted to communicate religious knowledge ; fo that, as the minifter is feldom
feen but in the pulpit (I mean in a minifterial character) all the opportunity that
the people have of being inftructed in the
theory of religion, is their hearing mifcel-
laneous difcourfes, which are now almoft e-
very where confined to fubjects, which have
an immediate relation to practice, while

the

the *theory of religion*, and the *evidences of it*, are almoſt wholly neglected.

Becauſe *common ſenſe* is a ſufficient guard againſt many errors in religion, it ſeems to have been taken for granted, that common ſenſe is a ſufficient *inſtructor* alſo ; whereas, in fact, without poſitive inſtruction, men would naturally have been mere *ſavages* with reſpect to religion ; as, without ſimilar inſtruction, they would be ſavages with reſpect to the arts of life and the ſciences. Common ſenſe can only be compared to a *judge* ; but what can a judge do without evidence, and proper materials from which to form a judgment.

Such is the *evil*, of which not myſelf only, but every perſon who ſeriouſly conſiders the preſent ſtate of things among the diſſenters, and its manifeſt tendency in futurity, complain. Let us now conſider what is the moſt proper and effectual *remedy* for this evil, and how far the application of it may be eaſy and practicable.

As the fource of the evil, as far as it arifes from ourfelves, was obferved to be two fold, namely the neglect of *parental* and *minifterial* inftruction, it is eafy to infer, that the moft complete and effectual remedy muft be two fold alfo, confifting in the revival of that difcipline, both in churches and private families, by which we ourfelves received that inftruction, the advantages of which we are apt to overlook, till we fee the dreadful effects of the want of it in others. If the difcipline of our forefathers, in either of thefe refpects, has been too fevere for the gentlenefs of modern manners, let that feverity be relaxed, but let nothing that is really ufeful be laid afide.

It is neceffary that more attention be given both to the morals and the religious inftruction of youth by thofe who undertake the conduct of our focieties, as well as by their parents. If it be impoffible, as I am apprehenfive it generally will be, to revive the ancient forms of our church difcipline, or to improve upon them (in
consequence

confequence of which a number of the moſt intelligent, ſerious, and prudent members of our churches might be appointed to ſuperintend the inſtruction of youth) let the miniſter exert himſelf the more in this field, which alone can promiſe a reward for his labours. When a perſon's mode of thinking, and his habits of life are fixed, as they generally are before they arrive at thirty or forty years of age, and eſpecially when they have been confirmed by having met with no oppoſition or controul, from that time to a more advanced period of life, there can be but little proſpect of making any good and laſting impreſſions. In this caſe, a change of thinking, or acting, will be brought about, if at all, with very great difficulty, and old notions and habits will be apt to return upon the ſlighteſt occaſions, and get firmer hold of the mind than ever.

If men have lived all their lives unacquainted with better principles, the propoſal of them may ſtrike and influence ;

but

but if they relate to fubjects which they have often heard canvaffed, and on which little can be faid that is abfolutely *new* to them, it may be taken for granted, that the recital of arguments which they prefume have been fully confuted, will only confirm them in their former prejudices. It is beft, therefore, to bear with the *aged*, and, in many cafes, with thofe who are advanced to middle life, and not without fome very urgent reafon, arifing from very particular circumftances, attempt the arduous, and almoft hopelefs tafk of rectifying their errors; though fomething more fhould be done towards reforming their conduct. But in youth the mind is flexible, opinions are unfixed, and habits not confirmed. At this time of life, therefore, arguments and expoftulations may have real weight, good principles and maxims may be recommended with effect; and a little feafonable affiftance may be fufficient to mould them to our wifh.

The

The great object of a minifter's chief attention being thus fixed, viz. upon the younger, and more teachable part of his congregation, it remains to be confidered in what manner their inftruction may be beft provided for. Now it appears to me, that the only effectual provifion for this purpofe is a courfe of regular and fyftematical inftruction. Every branch of knowledge is built on certain facts and principles ; and in order that thefe be fully and clearly underftood, they muft be delivered in a proper order, fo that one thing may moft naturally introduce another. In other words, no branch of knowledge, religion not excepted, can be taught to advantage but in the way of *fyftem*. Frightful as this word may found, it fignifies nothing but an orderly and regular fet of principles, beginning with the eafieft, and ending with the moft difficult, which, in this manner, are the moft eafily demonftrated. No perfon would ever think of teaching *Law* or *Medicine*, or any other branch of fcience in the manner in which religion is now generally

taught ;

taught; and as no perfon ever acquired a competent knowledge of Law, Medicine, or any other fcience by hearing declamatory difcourfes upon the fubject; fo neither can we reafonably expect that a juft and comprehenfive knowledge of religion fhould ever be communicated in the fame loofe and incoherent manner. Befides, it is now too much the fafhion to neglect public worfhip, and any fcheme of bufinefs or pleafure is thought to be a fufficient excufe for a perfon's abfenting himfelf from it, even on the Lord's-day; fo that this only means of inftruction, infufficient as it is for the purpofe, is becoming every day more uncertain; and it may be expected that lefs advantage will be made of it continually.

On thefe accounts, religious knowledge will never be communicated, with certainty and good effect, from the pulpit only. Thofe of the congregation who think themfelves already fufficiently knowing, will be difgufted with the repetition of elementary principles; to thofe who are,

extremely

extremely ignorant, it is not poſſible, in a formal diſcourſe, to ſpeak plainly and familiarly enough; and thoſe whoſe minds are not ſufficiently enlightened, and eſpecially thoſe whoſe prejudices are of long ſtanding, will be apt to take offence at the diſcovery of truths which it will be impoſſible for them to comprehend or receive.

There can be no hope, therefore, of doing any thing to good purpoſe, in this way, unleſs the miniſter can have an opportunity of diſcourſing to the young men by themſelves. He may then converſe with them familiarly on the fundamental principles of natural and revealed religion; he may ſay the ſame things over and over again, and change his form of expreſſion, in order to make himſelf perfectly underſtood; he may alſo illuſtrate what he advances by familiar inſtances, and examples, and ſet every thing of importance in a great variety of lights. Moreover, if they will ſubmit to it (which it will be greatly to their advantage to do)

he

he may *examine* them on the fubjects on which he has difcourfed, fo as to fatisfy himfelf whether they have perfectly underftood him, whether they retain in memory the facts and reafonings which he has advanced, and be fufficiently grounded in one thing before he proceeds to another. This method will alfo give him an opportunity of removing any difficulties, or anfwering any objections which may have occurred to them, or which may have been thrown in their way by other perfons. In fhort, I would advife a minifter to form the young men of his congregation from the age of 18 or 20 to about 30 into an *academical clafs*, and take the very fame methods to teach them the elements of religion, that he would do to teach them the rudiments of any branch of natural knowledge.

To make this bufinefs the eafier to the tutor, and the more advantageous to his pupils, it will be farther advifable, that he give his lectures from a fhort text or fyftem, written, or rather printed, that they

they may have an opportunity of perufing it, and of ftudying it when they are by themfelves, and thereby the better pre-pare themfelves for examination.

I do not give this advice at random, or from theory only; for I have, in a great meafure, carryed the fcheme which I am now recommending into execution; and I can affure my friends in the miniftry that, as far as my own experience is a guide, they may promife themfelves much plea-fure, and their pupils much advantage from the exercife.

If it can be made agreeable to the peo-ple, I would alfo advife that the minifter deliver the heads of his fyftem in a fet of regular difcourfes to the congregation at large, once in four or five years, that thofe perfons whom it may not be advifa-ble to admit to his familiar lectures, may have an opportunity of hearing fome ufe-ful topicks difcuffed, at leaft, in a concife manner, which they might, otherwife, have never heard of at all. But, if the

congregation

congregation fhould not be fufficiently
uniform in their fentiments, it will hardly
be prudent, for reafons fufficiently hinted
above, to adopt this meafure. It will
alfo depend upon particular circumftances, whether the *young women* fhould be
admitted to the familiar lectures along with
the young men, or not.

That my readers may perfectly underftand my fcheme, and derive what advantage they pleafe from it, I propofe, God
willing, to publifh all the heads of my own
lectures, under the title of *Inftitutes of na-*
tural and revealed religion. Minifters whofe
fentiments are pretty nearly my own may,
perhaps, fave themfelves fome trouble by
making ufe of them, departing from my
particular fentiments or method, whenever they think proper. The whole work
will be divided into four parts, the firft
comprizing the principles of natural religion, the fecond the evidences of revelation, the third the doctrine of revelation,
and the fourth an account of the corrup-
tions of chriftianity. This laft will contain

tain the reafons for our proteftant faith, and alfo thofe of our diffent from the eftablifhed church of England, with which every diffenter ought to be made thoroughly acquainted.

Befides this principal clafs, I would advife a minifter, who is defirous to communicate religious knowledge with effect, and who would adapt his inftructions to the different ages of his hearers, to form *two other claffes*, one confifting of children under fourteen years of age. To thefe he fhould teach a *fhort catechifm*, containing the firft elements of religious knowledge, delivered in the plaineft and moft familiar language poffible; and when it is made ufe of, a variety of other queftions fhould be afked, calculated to bring the fubject to the level of their capacities. A catechifm of this kind I publifhed fome years ago; and I am fatisfied, from my own experience, that a child, even of four or five years of age, may be made to underftand the moft important truths of chriftianity, and that it is of great confequence.

fequence that the minds of children be imprefled with this kind of knowledge. as early as poffible. No perfon who has actually made a trial of this method of inftructing children, and who can do it with any degree of judgment, will fay that it is a painful tafk to a child. On the contrary, I have generally found them to be pleafed, and in many cafes exceedingly delighted with it.

In the other junior clafs I would teach the knowledge of the *fcriptures* only. This appears to me to be a fubject fo diftinct, copious, and important, that a feparate clafs fhould be appropriated to it; and I think that the beft manner in which this great end can be gained, is to have a fet of *queftions only*, printed, with references to thofe places in the bible, which muft be read, in order to find the proper anfwers. Such a *fcripture catechifm* as this I have drawn up, and fhall immediately publifh for my own ufe, and that of thofe who may approve of it. This clafs may properly confift of young perfons of both fexes,

fexes, between the ages of fourteen and eighteen, or twenty, fo as to be an intermediate clafs, between the two others. It may be advifable, however, and may even be neceffary at the firft, to add to this clafs fuch members of the higher clafs as are not fufficiently acquainted with the fcriptures; and, in the prefent ftate of our focieties, I am afraid that many fuch will be found above twenty years of age; but of thefe it may be hoped that there will be many, who will not think themfelves too old to learn, and who may even take pleafure in fuch an exercife as this, which is equally calculated to improve the moft knowing, as well as to inftruct the moft ignorant.

Thefe three claffes appear to me to be fufficient for the purpofe of communicating religious inftruction; at leaft, I cannot, at prefent, think of any thing better adapted to the purpofe. I fincerely wifh that other minifters, who cannot but be fenfible of the evil that I complain of, would propofe what appears to them to be

be a proper remedy for it, and let us freely
adopt whatever we approve in each others
fchemes.

To make room for lectures of fuch
manifeft utility as thefe, which I have
now recommended, it were to be wifhed
that *weekly*, and other *periodical preaching
lectures*, efpecially that which is in many
places preparatory to the Lord's fupper,
were laid afide. The laft mentioned fer-
vice, whatever good it may do in other
refpects, does, unqueftionably, promote
fuperftition; continually fuggefting and
confirming the opinion, that the attend-
ance upon this chriftian ordinance requires
more particular preparation than any
other, which is an idea that could never
occur to any perfon in perufing the New
Teftament only, and can be nothing but
the remains of the popifh doctrine of
tranfubftantiation.

Other weekly or monthly fermons are
feldom attended except by a few perfons,
and thofe chiefly the aged, and fuch others
as

as have the leaft occafion for them ; and they are often a burden to the minifter, who is fenfible that he is giving his labour, which might be better beftowed, to very little purpofe. It has feemed fit to infinite wifdom, that one day in feven is proper and fufficient for reft from labour, and the purpofes of public worfhip. When we are got beyond this *fcripture directory*, all the reft is fuch *will worfhip*, as no bounds can be fet to. It has certainly been the foundation of much fuperftition, and has, in many cafes, occafioned a fatal and very criminal neglect of the proper bufinefs of this life. In what I have now faid I would by no means be underftood to condemn all occafional acts of public worfhip, as on days fet apart for public fafting and thankfgiving. or on particular annual folemnities, fome of which anfwer very good purpofes.

As all chriftians are brethren, and we are exprefsly commanded to *exhort one another,* I hope it will not be deemed arrogant in me to have given my advice with refpect to a matter of fo much importance, as the beft

beft method of communicating religious
knowledge, in which all chriftian minifters
are equally concerned. The fchemes
which I have propofed are fuch as I can
recommend from the trial that I have made
of them, and they appear to me to be very
practicable by any perfon who is fufficiently qualified to difcharge any other part
of the minifterial duty ; and in the *country*,
I believe, that fuch fervices will generally
be acceptable as well as ufeful. As to the
city, I am not fo well able to judge ; but if
I be not mifinformed, the connection between *minifter* and *people* is, in general, fo
flight, that fchemes which fuppofe much
perfonal refpect for the paftor on one fide,
and an affectionate concern for the people
on the other, can hardly be expected to
fucceed. The prevailing practice of a
London minifter preaching to one congregation in the morning, and to another in
the afternoon, when each of them is able
to provide for one (as in fact they half
provide for two) tends ftill farther to fink
the *minifter* into a mere *lecturer*, and to exclude the idea of every thing befides a
                                    ftipulated

ftipulated fum of money on the one fide, and mere *ftipulated duty* on the other. In fuch congregations one would think that the epiftles of Paul to Timothy and Titus were never read; and certainly the bufinefs of *ordination* in fuch places muft be a mere form or farce, without any meaning whatever.

Hoping that my prefumption in offering the preceding advice has not given offence, I fhall take the farther liberty to conclude with a word of exhortation, in which I fhall think myfelf equally concerned.

Since, My brethren in the chriftian miniftry, in the prefent ftate of church difcipline, fo unequal a fhare of the burden is fallen upon us, let us not, through defpair of doing every thing that ought to be done, think ourfelves excufable in attempting nothing. If we cannot poffibly warn all the unruly, comfort all the feeble minded, inftruct all the ignorant, confirm all the doubting, and feek and fave all

that

that are in danger of being loft, let us do all that we can in each of thefe branches of minifterial duty. Since, with refpect to the bufinefs of *admonition*, we are fo circumftanced, that we can but feldom attempt any thing with a profpect of fuccefs, let us do the more by way of *inftruction*, which is a field that is ftill open to us. If we cannot reclaim from vice, let us endeavour to inftill thofe principles which may prevent the commiffion of it, and to communicate that rational and ufeful knowledge, which is the only folid foundation of virtuous practice and good conduct in life.

If every man be a *fteward*, according to the ability and opportunity which God has given him of being ufeful to his fellow creatures, much more ought we to confider ourfelves in that light; and it is required of every fteward that he be faithful to his truft. The mafter under whom we act, and to whom we are immediately accountable, is the great *fhepherd and bifhop of fouls, Chrift Jefus.* Our inftructions are to
feed

feed his lambs, and *his sheep.* Let us see to it, then, that none of thofe who are committed to our care *perish for lack of knowledge.* If they will *die in their iniquity,* let us fo act under the melancholy profpect, that *their blood may not be required at our hands*; that we may, at leaft, *fave our own fouls,* if not *thofe that hear us.* When our Lord fhall return, and take account of his fervants, let it appear that we have diligently improved the talents with which we were intrufted, that of two we have made other two, and of five other five, &c. and then, and then only, fhall we *not be afhamed before him at his coming.*

THE CONTENTS.

The CONTENTS

OF THE

INSTITUTES.

VOL. I.

PART I.

OF the being and attributes of God. — page 1

SEC. I. *Of the exiſtence of God, and thoſe attributes which are deduced from his being conſidered as uncauſed himſelf, and the cauſe of every thing elſe.* 5

SEC. II. *Of thoſe attributes of the deity which are deduced from the conſideration of his being the original cauſe of all things.* 15

SEC. III.

The Contents.

Sec. III. *Of thofe attributes of the divine being which the confideration of his works leads us to afcribe to him.*   page 18

Sec. IV. *Of thofe attributes of God which are deduced from the confideration of his power, wifdom, and goodnefs jointly.* 38

Sec. V. *Of the properties of the divine goodnefs.* ——— ——— 45

Sec. VI. *Of the moral perfections of God deduced from his goodnefs.* ——— 56

PART II. *Of the duty, and future expectations of mankind.* ——— 66

Sec. I. *Of the rule of right and wrong.* 66

Sec. II. *Of the different objects of purfuit, and the different paffions and affections of men correfponding to them.* ——— 76

Sec. III. *Of the ruling paffion, and an eftimate of the propriety and value of the different purfuits of mankind.* ——— 84

§ 1. *Of*

The Contents.

§ 1. *Of the pleasures of sense.* 86

§ 2. *Of the pleasures of imagination.* 96

§ 3. *Of self interest.* ———— 100

§ 4. *Of the passions which arise from our social nature.* ———— ———— 109

§ 5. *Of the sympathetic affections.* 115

§ 5. *Of the relative duties.* 123

§ 6. *Of the Theopathetic affections.* 126

§ 7. *Of the obligation of conscience.* 133

Sec. IV. *Of the means of virtue.* 139

PART III. *Of the future expectations of mankind.* ———— ———— 152

Institutes of Religion.

PART I.

Of the being and attributes of God.

IN thefe Inftitutes I fhall endeavour to
explain *the principles of natural and revealed religion*; or to affign the reafons
why we acknowledge ourfelves to be fubject to the moral government of God, and
why we profefs ourfelves to be chriftians,
and confiftent proteftants.

Knowledge of this kind is, in its own
nature, the moft important of any that
we can give our attention to; becaufe it is

A   the

the moft nearly connected with our prefent and future happinefs.

If there be a God, and if we be accountable to him for our conduct, it muft be
highly interefling to us to know all that we
can concerning his character and government, concerning what he requires of us,
and what we have to expect from him.
If it be true that a perfon, pretending to
be fent from God, hath affured us of a
future life, it certainly behoves us to examine his pretentions to divine authority;
and if we fee reafon to admit them, to inform ourfelves concerning the whole of
his inftructions, and particularly what
kind of behaviour here will fecure our happinefs hereafter. Laftly, if the religion
we profefs be divine, and have been corrupted by the ignorance or artifice of men,
it is a matter of confequence that it be re-
ftored to its primitive purity; becaufe its
efficacy upon the heart and life muft depend upon it. And if men have ufurped
any power with refpect to religion which
the

the author of it has not given them, it is of confequence that their unjuft claims be expofed and refifted.

In order to give the moft diftinct view of the principles of religion, I fhall firft explain what it is that we learn from *na-ture*, and then what farther lights we receive from *revelation*. But it muft be obferved, that, in giving a delineation of natural religion, I fhall deliver what I fuppofe *might* have been known concerning God, our duty, and our future expectations by the light of nature, and not what *was actually* known of them by any of the human race; for thefe are very different things. Many things are, in their own nature, attainable, which, in fact, are never attained; fo that though we find but little of the knowledge of God, and of his providence, in many nations, which never enjoyed the light of revelation, it does not follow that nature did not contain and teach thofe leffons, and that men had not the means of learning them, provided

A 2 they

they had made the moſt of the light they had, and of the powers that were given them.

I ſhall, therefore, include under the head of *natural religion*, all that can be demonſtrated, or proved to be true by natural reaſon, though it was never, in fact, diſcovered by it; and even though it be probable that mankind would never have known it without the aſſiſtance of revelation. Thus the doctrine of a future ſtate may be called a doctrine of natural religion, if when we have had the firſt knowledge of it from divine revelation, we can afterwards ſhow that the expectation of it was probable from the light of nature, and that preſent appearances are, upon the whole, favourable to the ſuppoſition of it.

SECTION

SECTION I.

Of the exiſtence of God, and thoſe attributes which are deduced from his being conſidered as uncauſed himſelf, and the cauſe of every thing elſe.

WHEN we ſay there is a GOD, we mean that there is an intelligent deſigning cauſe of what we ſee in the world around us, and a being who was himſelf uncauſed. Unleſs we have recourſe to this ſuppoſition, we cannot account for preſent appearances ; for there is an evident incapacity in every thing we ſee of being the cauſe of its own exiſtence, or of the exiſtence of other things. Though, in one ſenſe, ſome things are the cauſes of others, yet they are only ſo in part ; and when we give ſufficient attention to their nature, we ſhall ſee, that it is very improperly that they are termed *cauſes* at all : for when we have allowed all that we can to their influence and ope-

ration,

ration, there is ſtill ſomething that muſt be referred to a prior and ſuperior cauſe. Thus we ſay that a proper ſoil, together with the influences of the ſun and the rain, are the cauſes of the growth of plants ; but, in fact, all that we mean, and all that, in ſtrictneſs, we ought to ſay, is, that according to the preſent conſtitution of things, plants could not grow but in thoſe circumſtances ; for, if there had not been a body previouſly organized like a plant, and if there had not exiſted what we call a *conſtitution of nature*, in conſequence of which plants are diſpoſed to thrive by the influence of the ſoil, the ſun, and the rain, thoſe circumſtances would have ſignified nothing ; and the fitneſs of the organs of a plant to receive nouriſhment from the ſoil, the rain, and the ſun, is a proof of ſuch wiſdom and deſign, as thoſe bodies are evidently deſtitute of. If the fitting of a ſuit of cloaths to the body of a man be an argument of *contrivance*, and conſequently prove the exiſtence of an intelligent agent, much more is the fitneſs

of

of a thoufand things to a thoufand other
things in the fyftem of nature a proof of
an intelligent defigning caufe; and this
intelligent caufe we call GOD.

If, for argument's fake, we fhould admit that the immediate author of this
world was not himfelf the firft caufe, but
that he derived his being and powers from
fome other being, fuperior to him; ftill
in tracing the caufe of this being, and the
caufe of his caufe, &c. we fhall at length
be conftrained to acknowledge a *firft caufe*,
one who is himfelf uncaufed, and who
derives his being and caufe from no fuperior whatever.

It muft be acknowledged, however, that
our faculties are unequal to the comprehenfion of this fubject. Being ufed to
pafs from effects to caufes, and being ufed
to look for a caufe adequate to the thing
caufed, and confequently to expect a
greater caufe for a greater effect, it is natural to fuppofe, that, if the things we

fee,

fee, which we fay are the production of divine power, required a caufe, the divine being himfelf muft have required a greater caufe. But this train of reafoning would lead us into a manifeft abfurdity, in inquiring for a higher and a higher caufe *ad infinitum*. It may, perhaps, be true, though we cannot diftinctly fee it to be fo, that as all *finite* things require a caufe, *infinites* admit of none. It is evident, that nothing can *begin* to be without a caufe ; but it by no means follows from thence, that that muft have had a caufe which had *no beginning*. But whatever there may be in this conjecture, we are conftrained, in purfuing the train of caufes and effects, to ftop at laft at fomething uncaufed.

That any being fhould be *felf created* is evidently abfurd, becaufe that would fuppofe that he had a being before he had, or that he exifted, and did not exift at the fame time. For want of clearer knowledge of this fubject, we are obliged

to content ourfelves with terms that convey only *negative* ideas, and to fay that
God is a being *uncreated,* or *uncaufed;* and
this is all that we mean when we fometimes fay that he is *felf exiftent.*

It has been faid by fome, that if we
fuppofe an *infinite fucceffion* of finite beings,
there will be no neceffity to admit any
thing to have been uncaufed. The race
of men, for inftance, may have been from
eternity, no individual of the fpecies being much fuperior to the reft. But this
fuppofition only involves the queftion in
more obfcurity, and does not approach,
in the leaft, to the folution of any difficulty. For if we carry this imaginary fucceffion ever fo far back in our ideas, we
are in juft the fame fituation as when we
fet out; for we are ftill confidering a fpecies of beings who cannot fo much as
comprehend even their own make and
conftitution; and we are, therefore, ftill
in want of fome being who was capable
of thoroughly knowing, and of forming

A 5   them,

them, and alſo of adapting the various parts of their bodies, and the faculties of their minds, to the ſphere of life in which they act. In fact, an infinite *ſucceſſion* of finite beings as much requires a cauſe, as a *ſingle* finite being ; and we have as little ſatisfaction in conſidering one of them as uncauſed, as we have in conſidering the other.

It was ſaid, by the Epicureans of old, that all things were formed by the *fortuitous coŋcourſe of atoms*, that, originally, there were particles of all kinds floating at random in infinite ſpace ; and that, ſince certain combinations of particles conſtitute all bodies, and ſince, in infinite time, theſe particles muſt have been combined in all poſſible ways, the preſent ſyſtem at length aroſe, without any deſigning cauſe. But, ſtill, it may be aſked, how could theſe atoms *move* without a *mover* ; and what could have ariſen from their combinations, but mere heaps of matter, of different forms and ſizes. They

They could, of themfelves, have had no power of acting upon one another, as bodies now have, by fuch properties as magnetifm, electricity, gravitation, &c. unlefs thefe powers had been communicated to them by fome fuperior being.

It is no wonder, that we feel, and muft acknowledge the imperfection of our faculties, when they are employed upon fuch a fubject as this. We are involved in inextricable difficulties in confidering the origin, as we may fay, of the *works* of God. It is impoffible that we fhould conceive how creation fhould have been coeval with its maker; and yet, if we admit that there ever was a time when nothing exifted, befides the divine being himfelf, we muft fuppofe a whole eternity to have preceded any act of creation; an eternity in which the divine being was poffeffed of the power and difpofition to create, and to make happy, without once exerting them; or that a reafon for creating muft have occurred to him after the lapfe

of

of a whole eternity, which had not occurred before; and theſe ſeem to be greater
difficulties than the other. Upon the
whole, it ſeems to be the moſt agreeable
to reaſon, though it be altogether incom-
prehenſible by our reaſon, that there never
was a time when this great uncauſed being
did not exert his perfections, in giving life
and happineſs to his offspring. We ſhall,
alſo, find no greater difficulty in admitting, that the creation, as it had no beginning, ſo neither has it any *bounds*; but
that infinite ſpace is repleniſhed with
worlds, in which the power, wiſdom, and
goodneſs of God always have been, and
always will be diſplayed.

There ſeems to be no difficulty in theſe
amazing ſuppoſitions, except what ariſes
from the imperfection of our faculties;
and if we reject theſe, we muſt of neceffity adopt other ſuppoſitions, ſtill more
improbable, and involve ourſelves in much
greater difficulties. It is, indeed, impoſ-
fible for us to conceive, in an adequate
manner,

manner, concerning any thing that is infinite, or even to exprefs ourfelves concerning them without falling into feeming abfurdities. If we fay that it is impoffible that the works of God fhould have been from eternity, we may fay the fame concerning any particular thought in the divine mind, or even concerning any particular moment of time in the eternity that has preceded us; for thefe are all of the nature of particular *events,* which muft have taken place at fome definite time, or at fome precife given diftance from the prefent moment. But as we are fure that the divine being himfelf, and *duration* itfelf, muft have been without beginning, notwithftanding this argument; the works of God may alfo have been without beginning, notwithftanding the fame argument. It may make this difficulty the eafier to us, to confider that *thinking* and *acting,* or *creating,* may be the fame thing with God.

So little are our minds equal to theſe
ſpeculations, that though we all agree,
that an infinite duration muſt have preceded the preſent moment, and that another infinite duration muſt neceſſarily follow it; and though the former of theſe is
continually receiving additions, which is,
in our idea, the ſame thing as its growing
continually larger; and the latter is con-
ſtantly ſuffering as great diminutions,
which, in our idea, is the ſame thing as
its growing continually leſs; yet we are
forced to acknowledge that they both ever
have been, and always muſt be exactly
equal; neither of them being at any time
conceivably greater, or leſs than the other.
Nay we cannot conceive how both theſe
eternities, added together, can be greater
than either of them ſeparately taken.

Having demonſtrated the exiſtence of
God, as the firſt cauſe, the creator, and
diſpoſer of all things; we are naturally
led to inquire, in the next place, what
properties or attributes he is poſſeſſed of.
Now

Now thefe naturally divide themfelves into *two claffes*; being either fuch as flow from his being confidered as the original caufe of all things, or fuch as the particular nature of the works of which he is the author lead us to afcribe to him.

SECTION II.

Of thofe attributes of the deity which are deduced from the confideration of his being the original caufe of all things.

SINCE matter is a fubftance incapable of moving itfelf; fince it can only be *acted upon*, and we cannot connect with it the idea of *action*, or an original power of acting upon other things, we cannot but conclude that God is an *immaterial* being, or a *fpirit*. But, we muft acknowledge ourfelves to be altogether ignorant of the nature or *effence* of God, and, indeed, of *matter* too; fince, to the properties of length, breadth, and thicknefs thickneſs, we cannot be certain but that other properties, of very different natures, ſuch as even *perception* and *intelligence*, may be ſuperadded. But ſhould this be poſſible, we ſtill cannot conceive that a thing which, of itſelf, is ſo ſluggiſh and inert, ſhould be the original cauſe and fountain of life, action, and motion to all other beings. Notwithſtanding our ignorance, therefore, concerning the nature of matter, and of the properties which may, or may not be compatible with it, there ſeems to be ſufficient reaſon to conclude, that the eſſence of God cannot be matter, but ſomething very different from it, which we therefore call immaterial, or ſpiritual.

Secondly, the original cauſe of all things muſt have been *eternal*; for, ſince nothing can begin to exiſt without a cauſe, if there ever had been a time when nothing exiſted, nothing could have exiſted at preſent.

Thirdly,

Thirdly, this original caufe muft likewife be *immutable,* or not fubject to change. We feem to require no other proof of this, than the impoffibility of conceiving whence a change could arife in a being uncaufed. If there was no caufe of his exiftence itfelf, it feems to follow, that there could be no caufe of a change in the manner of his exiftence; fo that whatever he was originally, he muft for ever continue to be. Befides, a capacity of producing a change in any being or thing, implies fomething prior and fuperior, fomething that can control, and that is incapable of being refifted; which can only be true of the fupreme caufe itfelf.

The immutability of the divine being, or his being incapable of being acted upon, or controlled by any other, is what we mean when we fay that he is an *independent* being, if by this term we mean any thing more than his being *uncaufed.*

SECTION

Inſtitutes of

SECTION III.

Of thoſe attributes of the divine being which the conſideration of his works leads us to aſcribe to him.

THAT God is *immaterial, eternal,* and *immutable,* follows neceſſarily, as we have ſeen, from his being *uncauſed*; but if we conſider the *effects* of which he is the cauſe, or, in other words, the *works* of which he is the author, we ſhall be led, to aſcribe to him other attributes, particularly thoſe of *power, wiſdom,* and *goodneſs*; and conſequently all the attributes which are neceſſarily connected with, or flow from them.

If we call a being *powerful,* when he is able to produce great effects, or to accompliſh great works, we cannot avoid aſcribing this attribute to God, as the author of every thing that we behold; and when

we

we confider the apparent greatnefs, variety, and extent of the works of God, in
the whole frame of nature; as in the fun,
moon, and ftars; in the earth which we
inhabit, and in the vegetables and animals which it contains, together with the
powers of reafon and underftanding poffeffed by man, we cannot fuppofe any effect
to which the divine power is not equal;
and therefore we are authorifed to fay that
it is *infinite*, or capable of producing any
thing, that is not in its own nature impoffible; fo that whatever purpofes the divine being forms, he is always able to
execute.

The *defigns* of fuch a being as this, who
cannot be controlled in the execution of
any of his purpofes, would be very obvi-
ous to us if we could comprehend his
works, or fee the iffue of them; but this
we cannot do with refpect to the works of
God, which are both incomprehenfible by
our finite underftandings, and alfo are not
yet compleated; for as far as they are fubject

ject to our infpection, they are evidently
in a progrefs to fomething more perfect.
Yet from the *fubordinate parts* of this
great machine of the univerfe, which we
can in fome meafure underftand, and
which are compleated ; and alfo from the
manifeft *tendency* of things, we may fafely
conclude, that the great defign of the divine being, in all the works of his hands,
was to produce happinefs.

That the world is in a ftate of improvement is very evident in the human fpecies,
which is the moft diftinguifhed part of it.
Knowledge, and a variety of improvements depending upon knowledge (all of
which are directly or indirectly fubfervient to happinefs) have been increafing
from the time of our earlieft acquaintance
with hiftory to the prefent ; and in the laft
century this progrefs has been amazingly
rapid. By means of increafing commerce,
the valuable productions of the earth become more equally diftributed, and by
improvements in agriculture they are continually

tinually multiplied, to the great advantage of the whole family of mankind.

It is partly in confequence of this improvement of the human fpecies, as we may call it, that the earth itfelf is in a ftate of improvement, the cultivated parts continually gaining ground on the uncultivated ones; by which means, befides many other advantages, even the inclemencies of the weather are, in fome meafure, leffened, and the world becomes a more healthy and pleafurable abode for its moft important inhabitants. If things proceed as they have done in thefe refpects, the earth will become a paradife, compared to what it was formerly, or with what it is at prefent.

It is a confiderable evidence of the goodnefs of God, that the inanimate parts of nature, as the furface of the earth, the air, water, falts, minerals, &c. are adapted to anfwer the purpofes of vegetable and animal life, which abounds

every

every where; and the former of theſe is evidently ſubſervient to the latter; all the vegetables that we are acquainted with either directly contributing to the ſupport of animal life, or being, in ſome other way, uſeful to it; and all animals are furniſhed with a variety of appetites and powers, which continually prompt them to *ſeek*, and enable them to *enjoy* ſome kind of happineſs.

It ſeems to be an evident argument that the author of all things intended the animal creation to be happy, that, when their powers are in their full ſtrength, and exerciſe, they are always happy; health and enjoyment having a natural and neceſſary connection through the whole ſyſtem of nature; whereas it can hardly be imagined, but that a malevolent being, or one who ſhould have made creatures with a deſign to make them miſerable, would have conſtituted them ſo, that when any creature was the moſt perfect, it would have been the moſt unhappy.

It

It agrees with the fuppofition of the benevolence of the divine being, that there is the moft ample provifion made for the happinefs of thofe creatures which are naturally capable of the moft enjoyment, particularly the human fpecies. We have a far greater variety and extent of powers, both of action and enjoyment, than any other inhabitants of the earth; and the world abounds with more fources of happinefs to us than to any other order of beings upon it. So perfectly adapted are the inanimate, the vegetable, and the animal world to the occafions and purpofes of man, that we may almoft fay, that every thing was made for our ufe; and though there are both plants and animals, which, in fome applications, are noxious to us, yet, in time, we come to find out their ufes, and learn to avail ourfelves of their extraordinary powers.

There are many things in the fyftem of nature, as tempefts, lightning, difeafes, and death, which greatly terrify and annoy

noy us, and which are often the occaſion of much pain and diſtreſs; but theſe evils are only partial; and when the whole ſyſtem, of which they are a part, and a neceſſary conſequence, is conſidered, it will be found to be, as far as we can judge, the beſt, and the moſt friendly to us upon the whole; and that no other *general laws*, which ſhould obviate and exclude theſe evils, would have been productive of ſo much happineſs. And it ſhould be a rule with us, when we are conſidering any particular thing in the ſyſtem of nature, to take in every thing that is neceſſarily connected with it, and every thing that we ſhould loſe if we were deprived of it; ſo that if, upon the whole, we ſhould, in that caſe, loſe more than we ſhould gain, we muſt pronounce the thing complained of to be beneficial to us, and ſhould thankfully bear the evil, for the ſake of the greater good that accompanies it. Fire, for inſtance, is the occaſion of a great deal of miſchief and diſtreſs in the world, but this is not to be compared with the be-

nefits

nefits that we derive from the ufe of that element.

It may be faid, indeed, that the divine being might have feparated thefe things, and, if he had been perfectly benevolent, might have given us the good unmixed with evil. But there are many pains and evils which are ufeful to us, and upon the whole give us a greater enjoyment of life, as being pains and evils in themfelves. It is a common obfervation, that many perfons are much happier, in a variety of refpects, in the prime of life, and efpecially towards the clofe of it, for the pains and the hardfhips they fuffered at their entrance upon it. The difficulties we meet with contribute to ftrengthen the mind, by furnifhing proper exercife both for our paffions and our underftandings, and they alfo heighten our relifh of the good that we meet with. The more attention we give to evils of all kinds, the more good do we fee to accompany them, or to follow them; fo that, for any thing that we

know

know, a better ſyſtem, that is, a ſyſtem abounding with more happineſs, could not have been made than this, even as it is at preſent; and much more if we ſuppoſe, what is very probable, a tendency to much greater happineſs in the completion of the whole ſcheme.

One of the greateſt and moſt ſtriking evils in the ſyſtem of nature, is that one animal ſhould be made to prey upon another, as lions, tygers, wolves, eagles, ſerpents, and other beaſts, birds, and inſects of prey; and, at firſt ſight, it might ſeem more agreeable to benevolence, to have formed no ſuch carnivorous creatures; as every animal would then have lived without fear or apprehenſion, and the world, as we are apt to imagine, would have been the ſcene of univerſal peace and joy. But this is the concluſion of a ſuperficial obſerver. For it may eaſily be demonſtrated, that there is more happineſs in the preſent ſyſtem than there would have been in that imaginary one; and, therefore

fore, that this conſtitution of things, notwithſtanding its inconveniences, muſt have appeared preferable in the eye of a benevolent being.

If all the ſpecies of animals had been ſuffered to multiply without interfering with one another, they would all have ſoon been involved in famine and diſtreſs ; and whenever they died, their carcaſſes would have infected the air, and have made it nauſeous and unhealthy ; whereas, at preſent, all animals have, in general, a ſufficiency of food; they ſuffer very little from the fear of danger ; while they are in their vigour, they are pretty well able to defend themſelves, or to provide for their ſafety by flight ; when they grow feeble, and life would become a burthen, they ſerve to ſupport the life and vigour of animals of a different ſpecies ; and the pangs of a ſudden and violent death are not ſo dreadful as thoſe that are occaſioned by lingering ſickneſs. If any animals die by a natural death, there are other

animals

animals enow, quadrupeds, birds, and infects, that are ready to ſeize upon the carcaſe ; and to them it is, in the moſt putrid ſtate, grateful and wholeſome food.

Man is a carnivorous animal, but it is happy for the animals which he lives upon that he is ſo. What a number of cows, and ſheep, and fowls, do we feed, attend upon, and make happy ; which, other-wiſe, would either have had no exiſtence at all, or a very miſerable one ; and what is a ſudden and unexpected death, com-pared with their previous enjoyment; with a life ſpent in far greater pleaſure and ſa-tisfaction than they could otherwiſe have known ?

Farther, all the evils we complain of are the reſult of what we call *general laws*, in conſequence of which the ſame events invariably follow from the ſame previous circumſtances; and without thoſe general laws, all would be uncertainty and confu-ſion. Thus it follows from the general

law

law of gravitation, that bodies heavier than the air will, when unsupported, fall to the ground. Now cannot we conceive that it is better, upon the whole, that this law of nature, which is productive of a thousand benefits every moment, and whereby the whole earth, and probably the whole universe is held together, should be preserved invariably, than that it should be suspended whenever any temporary inconvenience would arise from it; as whenever a man should step from a precipiece, to prevent his breaking his bones, or being dashed to pieces? If there were no general laws of nature, causing the same effects to follow from the same previous circumstances, there would be no exercise for the wisdom and understanding of intelligent beings; and, consequently, we should not be in circumstances in which we could arrive at the proper perfection and happiness of our natures. If there were no general laws, we could not know what events to expect, or depend upon, in consequence of any thing

we

we did. We could have none of that pleafure and fatisfaction that we now have in contemplating the courfe of nature, which might be one thing to day, and another to morrow ; and as no man could lay a fcheme with a profpect of accomplifhing it, we fhould foon become liftlefs and indifferent to every thing, and confequently unhappy.

It may be faid, that we might have been differently conftituted, fo as to have been happy in a world not governed by general laws, and not liable to partial evils. But there is no end of thofe fuppofitions, which, for any thing that we can tell, may be, in their own nature, impoffible. All that we can do, in thefe difficult fpeculations, is to confider the connections and tendencies of things as they now are ; and if we fee reafon to conclude that, *ceteris manentibus*, nothing could be changed for the better, we may alfo conclude that the *fyftem itfelf* could not be changed for a better ; fince the fame wifdom that has fo
perfectly,

perfectly adapted the various parts of the fame fcheme, fo as to make it productive of the moft happinefs, may well be fuppofed to have made choice of *the fcheme itfelf,* as calculated to contain the moft happinefs. Even divine power cannot produce impoffibilities; and for any thing that we know, it may be as naturally impoffible to execute any fcheme free from the inconveniences, that we complain of in this, as that *two and two* fhould make more than *four.*

Upon the whole, the face of things is fuch as gives us abundant reafon to conclude, that God made every thing with a view to the happinefs of his creatures and offspring. And we are confirmed in this fuppofition, from confidering the utter impoffibility of conceiving of any end that could be anfwered to himfelf in the mifery of his creatures; whereas the divine being may be conceived to rejoice in, and perhaps receive pleafure from the happinefs of all around him. This, how-

ever,

ever, is the moſt *honourable* idea that we
can form of any being; and can it be ſuppoſed that our maker would have conſtituted us in ſuch a manner, as that our
natural ideas of perfection and excellence
ſhould not be applicable to the eſſential
attributes of his own nature? Our natural
approbation of love and benevolence is,
therefore, a proof of the divine benevolence, as it cannot be ſuppoſed that he
ſhould have made us to hate, and not to
love himſelf.

That every part of ſo complex a ſyſtem
as this ſhould be ſo formed, as to conſpire
to promote this one great end, namely
the happineſs of the creation, is a clear
proof of the *wiſdom* of God. The proper evidence of *deſign*, or *contrivance* is
ſuch a fitneſs of means to gain any end,
that the correſpondence between them
cannot be ſuppoſed to be the reſult of
what we call *accident*, or *chance*. Now
there are ſo many adaptations of one thing
to another in the ſyſtem of nature, that
the

the idea of chance is altogether excluded; infomuch that there is reafon enough to conclude, that every thing has its proper ufe, by means of a defigned reference to fomething elfe; and that nothing has been made, or is difpofed of, but to anfwer a good and benevolent purpofe. And the more clofely we infpect the works of God, the more exquifite art and contrivance do we difcover in them. This is acknowledged by all perfons who have made any part of nature their particular ftudy, whether they have been of a religious turn of mind, or not.

We fee the greateft wifdom in the diftribution of light and heat to the different parts of the earth, by means of the revolution of the earth upon its axis, and its obliquity to the plane in which it moves; fo that every climate is not only habitable by men whofe conftitutions are adapted to it, but every part of the world may be vifited by the inhabitants of any other place; and there is no country which the

fame

ſame perſon is not capable of accuſtoming himſelf to, and making tolerable, if not agreeable to him, in a reaſonable ſpace of time.

We ſee the greateſt wiſdom in the vari‑ ation of the ſeaſons of the year in the ſame place, in the proviſion that is made for watering as well as warming the ſoil, ſo as to prepare it for the growth of the vari‑ ous kinds of vegetables that derive their nouriſhment from it. The wiſdom of God appears in adapting the conſtitutions of vegetables and animals to the climates they were intended to inhabit, in giving all animals the proper means of providing their food, and the neceſſary powers ei‑ ther of attacking others, or ſecuring them‑ ſelves by flight, or ſome other method of evading the purſuit of *their* enemies. The carnivorous and voracious animals have a degree of ſtrength and courage ſuited to their occaſions, whereby they are prompted to ſeize upon their prey, and are enabled to maſter and ſecure it; and

the

the weak have that degree of timidity, which keeps them attentive to every appearance of danger, and warns them to have recourse to some methods of securing themselves from it. We see the greatest wisdom in the provision that is made in nature against the loss or extinction of any species of vegetables or animals, by their easy multiplication, according to the want there is of them. The most useful vegetables grow every where, without care or cultivation, as for example, the different kinds of grass. Small and tame animals breed fast, whereas the large and carnivorous ones propagate very slowly, which keeps the demand on the one hand, and the consumption on the other, nearly equal.

The human body exhibits the clearest and the most numerous marks of wisdom and contrivance, whereby each part receives its proper nourishment, and is fitted for its proper functions; all of which are admirably adapted to our real occasions

B 6. in

in life. How conveniently are the organs of all our ſenſes diſpoſed, how well ſecured, and how excellently adapted to their proper uſes; and how exceedingly ſerviceable are all of them to us. We ſee the wiſdom of God both in what we call the *inſtinEts* of brutes, and the *reaſon* of man; each of theſe principles being exactly fitted to our ſeveral occaſions.

We alſo ſee the wiſdom of God in the natural *ſanEtions of virtue* in this world; ſo that thoſe perſons who addiĉt themſelves to vice and wickedneſs become miſerable and wretched in the natural courſe of things, without any particular interpoſition of providence; whereas virtue and integrity is generally rewarded with peace of mind, the approbation of our fellow creatures, and a reaſonable ſhare of ſecurity and ſucceſs.

Could we ſee all the cauſes of the riſe and fall of empires, and in what manner the happineſs of mankind is connected with

with great events in the hiftory of the
world, it is not to be doubted, but that
we fhould fee as much wifdom in the conduct of divine providence with refpect to
them ; fo as not to doubt (though we
fhould not have been informed of it by
revelation) *that the Lord God ruleth in the
kingdoms of men, giving them to whomfoever
he pleafes,* and promoting his own wife
and benevolent purpofes by the difpofition of them.

Laftly, it is an argument of the wifdom of God, that he has given wifdom to
man and other creatures, for he could not
give a power of which he was not himfelf
poffeffed in a much more eminent degree.

Thefe attributes of *power*, *wifdom* and
goodnefs, are all that we can *directly* de-
monftrate from the confideration of the
works of God. Every other of his attributes is deduced from thefe ; and fince
the divine being has been proved to be
powerful, wife, and good, he muft likewife

wiſe be whatever a powerful, wiſe, and good being cannot but be. Theſe, there- fore, together with the attributes of *ſelf - exiſtence, immateriality, eternity*, and *un- -changeableneſs*, may be called the *primary* attributes of God; and all others may be called *ſecondary* ones, or ſuch as depend upon, and flow from thoſe that are pri- mary.

SECTION IV.

Of thoſe attributes of God which are deduced from the conſideration of his power, wiſ- dom, and goodneſs jointly.

AS the matter of which the world con- ſiſts can only be moved and acted upon, and is altogether incapable of mov- ing itſelf, or of acting; ſo all the *powers of nature*, or the tendencies of things to their

their different motions and operations, can only be the effect of the divine energy, perpetually acting upon them, and caufing them to have certain tendencies and effects. A ftone, for inftance, can no more move, or tend downwards, that is towards the earth, of itfelf, than it can move or tend upwards, that is from the earth. That it does tend downwards, or towards the earth, muft, therefore, be owing to the divine energy, an energy without which the power of gravitation would ceafe, and the whole frame of the earth be diffolved.

It follows from thefe principles, that no powers of nature can take place, and that no creature whatever can exift, without the divine agency; fo that we can no more *continue*, than we could *begin* to exift without the divine will.

God, having made all things, and exerting his influence over all things, muft know all things, and confequently be *omnifcient*

omniscient. Also, since he not only or-
dained, but constantly supports all the
laws of nature, he must be able to foresee
what will be the result of them, at any
distance of time; just as a man who makes
a clock can tell when it will strike. All
future events, therefore, must be as perfectly known to the divine mind as those
that are present; and as we cannot conceive that he should be liable to forgetful-
ness, we may conclude that all things,
past, present, and to come, are equally
known to him, so that his knowledge is
infinite.

The divine being, knowing all things,
and exerting his influence on all the works
of his hands, whereby he supports the
existence of every thing that he has made,
and maintains the laws which he has esta-
blished in nature, must be, in a proper
sense of the term, *omnipresent.* For, tho'
being a *spirit,* he can have no proper relation to place, and much less to one
particular place more than another (which

is

is a property of fpirit of which we can
have no adequate conception) he muft
have a power of acting every where, to
which the idea belonging to omniprefence
is fufficiently applicable.

Since God made all things to anfwer
an important end, namely the happinefs
of his creatures; fince his power is fo
great, that nothing can be too difficult for
him; fince his knowledge is fo extenfive,
that nothing can pafs unnoticed by him;
and fince the minuteft things in the creation, and the moft inconfiderable events,
may affect the end that he has in view, his
providence muft necefarily extend to all
his works; and we may conclude that he
conftantly attends to every individual of
his creatures, and out of every evil that
befalls any of them produces good to
themfelves or others.

We cannot help conceiving that any being muft be *happy* when he accomplifhes
all his defigns. The divine being, therefore,

fore, having power and wiſdom to execute all his deſigns, we infer that he muſt
be happy, and perfectly ſo. Alſo, though
we cannot ſay that the conſequence is de-
monſtrable, we cannot but think that he
who makes us happy, and whoſe ſole end
in creating us was to make us happy,
muſt be happy himſelf, and in a greater
degree than we are capable of being.

In all the preceding courſe of reaſoning, we have only argued from what we
ſee, and have ſuppoſed nothing more than
is neceſſary to account for what we ſee;
and as *a* cauſe is neceſſary, but not *more
cauſes* than one, we cannot conclude that
there are more Gods than *one*, unleſs ſome
other kind of proof can be brought for it.

Beſides, there is ſuch a perfect *harmony*
and *uniformity* in the works of nature, and
one part ſo exactly fits and correſponds to
another, that there muſt have been a perfect *uniformity of deſign* in the whole,
which hardly admits of more than one
being

being as the former of it, and prefiding over it. It was only the mixture of evil in the world that was the reafon why fome of the heathens fuppofed that there are *two principles* in nature, the one the fource of good, and the other of evil, the one benevolent, and the other malevolent.

Thefe two principles, they fuppofed to be at prefent continually ftruggling againft one another, though it was their opinion that the good would finally prevail. But we have feen that all the evil that there is in the world is a neceffary part of the whole fcheme, and infeparable from it; fo that the good and the evil muft have had the fame author. Befides, they both confpire to the fame end, the happinefs of the creation.

Upon the whole, we may remain per-fectly fatisfied, that there is but *one God*, poffeffed of all the perfections, that have been defcribed ; and were our minds equal to this fubject, I doubt not but that we fhould ſhould be able to ſee, that there *could have been* but one, and that two Gods would have been impoſſible; as much ſo, as that there ſhould be in nature two univerſal infinite ſpaces, or two eternities, both before and after the preſent moment. But becauſe we are incapable of judging what *muſt have been* in this caſe, we are content to argue from what *is*; and upon this ground we have reaſon enough to conclude that *God is one.*

Since the divine power and wiſdom are ſo amazingly great, that we cannot conceive any effect to which they are not equal; nay ſince we are *able to comprehend but* a very ſmall part of the actual effects of the power and wiſdom of God, and new views are continally opening to us, which are continually exciting greater admiration, there can be no danger of our exceeding the truth, if we endeavour to conceive of theſe perfections of God as *infinite.* Indeed we have ſufficient reaſon to believe that, ſtrictly ſpeaking, they
are

are fo; though we are not able directly to demonstrate it: becaufe we, being finite, cannot comprehend any thing that is infinite; and not being able to comprehend an infinite effect, we cannot fully demonstrate infinity in the caufe. The *extent*, and other properties of the divine goodnefs, I fhall confider more at large.

SECTION V.

Of the properties of the divine goodnefs.

IF goodnefs, or benevolence, be the great governing principle, or fpring of action in the divine being, happinefs muft prevail amongft thofe of his creatures that are capable of it. If it were poffible that there fhould be, upon the whole, more mifery than happinefs in the creation, it would be an argument that the fupreme being

being was malevolent. For ſince all ʃ tendencies and iſſues of things were, fr‹ the firſt, perfectly known to him, ɪ would, ſuppoſing him to be benevolent, have produced no· ſyſtem at all, rather than one in which miſery might prevail. No ſcheme, therefore, which ſuppoſes the greater number of the creatures of God to be miſerable upon the whole, can be conſiſtent with the ſuppoſition of the divine benevolence. The *means*, or the *manner* by which the creatures of God are involved in miſery makes no difference in this caſe ; for if it ariſe even from themſelves, it ariſes from the nature that God has given them ; and if he had foreſeen that the conſtitution which he gave them would, in the circumſtances in which he placed them, iſſue in their final ruin, he would not have given them that conſtitution, or have diſpoſed of them in that manner ; unleſs he had intended that they ſhould be finally miſerable ; that is, unleſs he himſelf had taken pleaſure in miſery, in conſequence of his being of a malevolent diſpoſition.— It

It muſt be impoſſible, for the ſame reaſon, that the divine being ſhould be capable of ſacrificing the intereſts of a *greater number*, to that of a *few* of his creatures; though it may, perhaps, be neceſſary, that the intereſts of a few give place to that of a greater number. For if he had a deſire to produce happineſs *at all*, it ſeems to be an evident conſequence, that he muſt prefer a greater degree of happineſs to a leſs; and a greater ſum of happineſs can exiſt in a greater number, than in a ſmaller.

For the ſame reaſon, alſo, the goodneſs of God muſt be *impartial*. Since the ſupreme being ſtands in an equal relation to all his creatures and offspring, he muſt be incapable of that kind of partiality, by which we often give the preference to one perſon above another. There muſt be a good reaſon for every thing that looks like *preference* in the conduct and government of God; and no reaſon can be a good one, with reſpect to a benevo-

lent

lent being, but what is founded upon benevolence. If, therefore, ſome creatures enjoy more happineſs than others, it muſt be becauſe the happineſs of the creation in general requires that they ſhould have that preference, and becauſe a leſs *ſum of good* would have been produced upon any other diſpoſition of things.

Thus it is probable that a *variety* in the ranks of creatures, whereby ſome have a much greater capacity of happineſs than others, and are therefore more favoured by divine providence than others, makes a *better ſyſtem*, and one more favourable to general happineſs, than any other, in which there ſhould have been a perfect equality in all advantages and enjoyments. We are not, therefore, to ſay that God is partial to men, becauſe they have greater powers, and enjoy more happineſs than worms ; but muſt ſuppoſe, that the ſyſtem in which there was proviſion for the greateſt ſum of happineſs requir-

ed

ed that there fhould be fome creatures in the rank of men, and others in the rank of worms; and that each has reafon to rejoice in the divine goodnefs, though they partake of it in different degrees. Indeed, it were abfurd to fuppofe, that, properly fpeaking, there was any thing like *preference* in the divine being chufing to make *this* a man, and *the other* a worm; becaufe they had no being before they were created; and therefore it could not be any thing like affection to the one more than the other that determined his conduct. In reality, it is improper to fay that God chofe to make *this a man*, and *that a worm*; for the proper expreffion is, that he chofe to make *a man*, and *a worm*.

Among creatures of the fame general clafs or rank, there may be differences in advantages and in happinefs; but they muft be founded on the fame confiderations with the differences in the ranks themfelves; that is, it muft be favourable to the happinefs of the whole that there

C fhould

ſhould be thoſe differences; and it cannot ariſe from any arbitrary or partial preference of one to another, independent of a regard to the happineſs of the whole; which is what we mean by an arbitrary and partial affection.

There is a variety of caſes in which we may plainly ſee, that the happineſs of one has a reference to, and is productive of the happineſs of others; as in the principle of benevolence, whereby we are naturally diſpoſed to rejoice in the happineſs of others. For we cannot procure ourſelves theſe ſympathetic pleaſures, at leaſt, in any conſiderable degree, without contributing to the happineſs of thoſe around us. This, being a ſource of pleaſure to ourſelves, is a conſtant motive to benevolent actions.

Laſtly, if God be benevolent at all, he muſt be *infinitely* ſo; at leaſt we can ſee no reaſon why he ſhould wiſh to make his creation happy *at all*, and not wiſh to

make

make it as happy *as poffible.* If this be the cafe, the reafon why all his creatures are not, at all times, as happy as their natures can bear, muft be becaufe *variety* and *a gradual advance* are, in the nature of things, neceffary to their complete and final happinefs.

Befides, as there is reafon to believe that the other perfections of God, his wifdom, power, &c. are infinite, it feems to follow, by analogy, that his goodnefs muft be fo too, though we may not be able to prove it demonftrably and confequentially.

It muft be owned to be impoffible completely to anfwer every objection that may be made to the fuppofition of the infinite benevolence of God; for, fuppofing all his creatures to be conftantly happy, ftill, as there are *degrees of happinefs*, it may be afked, why, if their maker be infinitely benevolent, do not his creatures enjoy a higher degree of it. But this queftion

may

may always be aſked, ſo long as the happineſs of any creature is only *finite*, that
is leſs than infinite, or leſs than the happineſs of God himſelf, which, in its own
nature, it muſt neceſſarily be. It muſt be
conſiſtent, therefore, even with the infinite
benevolence of God, that his creatures,
which are neceſſarily finite, be finitely,
that is imperfectly happy. And when all
the circumſtances relating to any being are
conſidered at once, as they are by the divine mind, poſitive evils have only the
ſame effect as a diminution of poſitive
good, being balanced, as it were, againſt
a degree of good to which it was equivalent; ſo that the overplus of happineſs
which falls to the ſhare of any being, after
allowance has been made for the evils
which he ſuffers, is to be conſidered as
his ſhare of *unmixed happineſs.*

It is only owing to our imperfection,
or the want of *comprehenſion of mind*, in
which, however, we advance every day,
that we are not able to make all our pleaſures

fures and pains perfectly to *coalefce*, fo as that we fhall be affected by the difference only. And whenever we fhall be arrived at this ftate; whenever, by long experience, we fhall be able to connect in our minds the ideas of all the things which are caufes and effects to one another; all partial evils will abfolutely vanifh in the contemplation of the greater good with which they are connected. This will be perfectly the cafe with refpect to all *intellectual* pleafures and pains, and even *painful fenfations*, will be much moderated, and more tolerable under the lively perfuafion of their contributing to our happinefs on the whole. However, in the light in which the divine being, who has this perfect comprehenfion, views his works, (and this muft be the true light in which they ought to be confidered) there is this perfect coincidence of all things that are connected with, and fubfervient to one another; fo that, fince all evils are necef-farily connected with fome good, and generally are directly productive of it, all the

works

works of God, appear to him *at all times*
very good, happineſs greatly abounding
upon the whole. And ſince the works
of God are infinite, he contemplates an
infinity of happineſs, of his own production, and, in his eye, happineſs unmixed
with evil.

This concluſion, however, is hardly
conſiſtent with the ſuppoſition that any of
the creatures of God are neceſſarily miſerable in the whole of their exiſtence. In
the ideas of ſuch creatures, even when
they have arrived at the moſt perfect comprehenſion of mind, their being muſt ſeem
a curſe to them, and the author of it will
be conſidered as malevolent with reſpect
to them, though not ſo to others.

It ſeems, likewiſe, to be a reflection
upon the *wiſdom* of God, that he ſhould
not be able to produce the happineſs of
ſome, without the final miſery of others;
and ſo incapable are we of conceiving
how the latter of theſe can be neceſſary

to

to the former; that, if we retain the idea of the divine benevolence, together with his power and wifdom in any high degree, we cannot but reject the fuppofition. That any of the creatures of God fhould be finally, and upon the whole, miferable, cannot be a pleafing circumftance to their benevolent author; nay it muft, in its own nature, be the laft means that he would have recourfe to, to gain his end; becaufe, as far as it prevails, it is directly oppofed to his end. We may, therefore reft fatisfied, that there is no fuch *blot* in the creation as this; but that all the creatures of God are intended by him to be happy upon the whole. He ftands in an equal relation to them all, a relation in which they muft all have reafon to rejoice. He is their common father, protector, and friend.

SECTION

SECTION VI.

Of the moral perfections *of God deduced from his goodneſs.*

THE power and wiſdom of God, together with thoſe attributes which are derived from them, and alſo thoſe which are deduced from his being conſidered as an uncauſed being, may be termed his *natural* perfections; whereas his benevolence, and thoſe other attributes which are deduced from it, are more properly termed his *moral* perfections; becauſe they lead to ſuch conduct as determines what we commonly call *moral character* in men.

The ſource of all the moral perfections of God ſeems to be his benevolence; and indeed there is no occaſion to ſuppoſe him

to

to be influenced by any other principle, in order to account for all that we fee. Every other truly venerable or amiable attribute can be nothing but a *modification* of this. A perfectly good, or benevolent being, muft be, in every other refpect, whatever can be the object of our reverence, or our love. Indeed the connection of all the moral virtues, and the derivation of them from the fingle principle of benevolence are eafily traced, even in human characters.

1. If a magiftrate be benevolent, that is, if he really confult the happinefs of his fubjects, he muft be *juft*, or take notice of crimes, and punifh the criminals. Otherwife, he would be cruel to the whole, and efpecially to the innocent, who would be continually liable to oppreffion, if there were no reftraint of this kind.

2. But whenever an offence can be overlooked, and no injury accrue from it,

either

either to the offender himfelf, or to others, the benevolence of God, as well as that of a human magiftrate, will require him to be *merciful*; fo that implacability, or a defire of revenging an affront, without any regard to the prevention of farther evil, muft be carefully excluded from the character of the divine being. He muft delight in mercy becaufe he wifhes to promote happinefs, though he may be under a neceffity of punifhing obftinate offenders, in order to reftrain vice and mifery.

There is more room for the difplay of mercy in the divine government than in that of men; becaufe men, not being able to diftinguifh true repentance from the appearances of it, and pretences to it, muft make but few deviations from general rules, left they fhould increafe crimes and hypocrify; whereas the fecrets of all hearts being open to God, he cannot be impofed upon by any pretences; fo that if an offender be truly penitent, and it is known to him that he will not abufe his

goodnefs,

goodnefs, he can receive him into favour, without apprehending any, inconvenience whatever. Such cafes as thefe, how dangerous foever the precedent might be in human governments, are not liable to be abufed in the perfect adminiftration of the divine being. Juftice and mercy, therefore, are equally attributes of the divine being, and equally deducible from his goodnefs or benevolence; both, in their places, being neceffary to promote the happinefs of his creation.

3. As perfect benevolence is the rule of the divine conduct, and leads him to be both juft and merciful, fo we cannot but conceive that he muft govern his conduct by every other rule that we find to be equally neceffary to the well-being of fociety, particularly that of truth, or *veracity*. All human confidence would ceafe if we could not depend upon one another's word; and, in thofe circumftances, every advantage of fociety would be loft. There can be no doubt, therefore, but that the

divine

divine being, if he ſhould think proper to
have any intercourſe with his creatures,
muſt be equally removed from a poſſibility of attempting to impoſe upon them.

4. As to thoſe vices which ariſe from
the irregular indulgence of our appetites
and paſſions, we can have no idea of the
poſſibility of their having any place in the
divine being. We therefore conclude that
he is, in all reſpects, *holy*, as well as juſt
and good.

There are, alſo, ſome evidences of the
juſtice and mercy of God in the courſe of
providence. The conſtitution of human
nature and of the world is ſuch, that men
cannot long perſiſt in any ſpecies of wickedneſs without being ſufferers in conſequence of it. Intemperance lays the
foundation for many painful and dangerous diſeaſes. Every ſpecies of malevolence and inhumanity conſiſts of uneaſy
ſenſations, and expoſes the perſon in whom
they are predominant to the hatred and ill
offices

offices of his fellow creatures. Want of veracity deftroys a man's credit in fociety; and all vices, in general, make men fubject to contempt, or diflike; whereas the habitual practice of the contrary virtues promotes health of body and peace of mind; and in general, they infure to him the efteem and good offices of all thofe with whom he is connected.

Now, fince thefe evils which attend upon vice, and this happinefs which refults from virtue are the divine appointment (fince they take place in confequence of his conftitution of the courfe of nature) they may be confidered as the natural punifhments of vice, and the natural rewards of virtue, diftributed according to the rules of juftice and equity, and intended to inculcate the moft ufeful moral leffons on all his intelligent offspring, the fubjects of his moral government.

We, alfo, fee fomething like the exercife of *mercy* in the conduct of the divine provi-

providence; ſince the natural puniſhments of vice ſeldom take place immediately, but leave a man room to recollect, and recover himſelf; and, if, after a man *has* been addicted to vice, he become truly reformed, the inconveniences he has brought upon himſelf are, in general, either removed, or mitigated; ſo that he finds his condition the better for it.

It may, alſo, according to the reaſoning applied in a former caſe, be conſidered as an argument for all the perfections of God, that we are ſo formed, that we cannot but approve of, and eſteem every branch of virtue, For it cannot be ſuppoſed that our maker would have formed us in ſuch a manner, as that he himſelf ſhould be the object of our diſlike and abhorrence. Our natural love of goodneſs and virtue, therefore, is a proof that every branch of it enters into the character of the divine being, and conſequently that thoſe qualities are the objects of his favour and approbation.

Since,

Since, however, all the moral perfections of God are derived from his benevolence; fo that holinefs, juftice, mercy,
and truth, are in him only modifications,
as it were, of fimple goodnefs; we fhould
endeavour to conceive of him, as much
as poffible, according to his real nature;
confidering benevolence as his fole ruling
principle, and the proper fpring of all
his actions. This is, alfo, the moft *honourable* and the moft *amiable* light in
which we can view him, remembering
that goodnefs neceffarily implies what we
call juftice, though its more natural form
be that of mercy,

Upon the whole, it muft be acknowledged, that it is but a very imperfect
idea that we can form of the *moral* perfections of God from the light of nature.
It hardly amounts to what may be called
an idea of his *character.* We know nothing of God by the light of nature, but
through the medium of his works; and
thefe are fuch as we cannot fully comprehend;

hend ; both the efficient and the final
cauſes being, in many caſes, unknown to
us : whereas the clearer ideas we have of
the characters of men are acquired from
a reflection upon ſuch parts of their conduct as we can both fully comprehend,
and are capable of ourſelves ; ſo that we
can tell preciſely how we ſhould *feel* and
be diſpoſed, if we acted in the ſame manner. The knowledge, alſo, of the *manner in which men expreſs themſelves*, upon
known occaſions, is a great help to us in
judging of what they feel, and conſequently in inveſtigating their proper character ; and this is an advantage of which
we are intirely deſtitute, with reſpect to
God, on the principles of the light of nature. It is from *revelation* chiefly, if not
only, that we get a juſt idea of what we
may call the proper character of the divine
being. There we may both hear his declarations, and ſee various ſpecimens of
his conduct, with reſpect to a variety of
perſons and occaſions ; by which means
we have the beſt opportunity of entering,

as

as it were, into his fentiments, perceiving his difpofition, learning what are the objects of his approbation or diflike, in fhort, of gaining a proper and diftinct idea of his *moral character.*

PART

PART II.

OF THE DUTY, AND FUTURE EXPECTA-
TIONS OF MANKIND.

SECTION I.

Of the rule of right and wrong.

HAVING ſeen what it is that nature teaches us concerning GOD,
our next inquiry reſpects the proper *rule
of human conduct*, and our *expectations*,
grounded upon that conduct. No man
comes into the world to be idle. Every
man is furniſhed with a variety of paſſions,
which will continually engage him in ſome
purſuit or other; and the great queſtion
we have to decide is what paſſions we
ought to indulge, and what purſuits we
ought

ought to engage in. Now there are feveral very proper rules by which to form our judgment in this cafe ; becaufe there are feveral juft objects that we ought to have in view in our conduct. It is very happy, however, that this variety in our views can never miflead us, fince all the great ends we ought to keep in view are all gained by the fame means. They are, therefore, like fo many different clues to lead to the fame end ; and in the following inquiry I fhall make ufe of any one of them, or all of them, as it may happen that, in any particular cafe, they can be applied to the moft advantage.

Strictly fpeaking, there are no more than two juft and independent rules of human conduct, according to the light of nature, one of which is obedience to the will of God, and the other a regard to our own real happinefs ; for another rule, which is a regard to the good of others, exactly coincides with a regard to the will of God; fince all that we know of the

will

will of God, according to the light of
nature, is his desire that all his creatures
ſhould be happy, and therefore that they
ſhould all contribute to the happineſs of
each other. In revelation we learn the
will of God in a more direct method, and
then obedience to God, and a regard to
the good of others will be diſtinct and
independent principles of action, though
they both enjoin the ſame thing. The
fourth, and laſt rule of human conduct,
is a regard to the dictates of *conſcience.*
But this is only the ſubſtitute of the other
principles, and, in fact, ariſes from them;
prompting to right conduct on emergencies, where there is no time for reaſoning
or reflection; and where, conſequently,
no proper rule of conduct could be applied.

Having thus pointed out the proper
diſtinction and connection of theſe rules,
I ſhall conſider each of them ſeparately.
The firſt object of inquiry, in order to in-
veſtigate the proper rule of right and
wrong

wrong, is what kind of conduct the divine being most approves.

Now the divine being, whose own object, as has been shewn, is the happiness of his creatures, will certainly most approve of those sentiments, and of that conduct of ours, by which that happiness is best provided for; and this conduct must deserve to be called *right* and *proper* in the strictest sense of the words. If we examine the workmanship of any artist, our only rule of judging of what is right or wrong, with respect to it, is its fitness to answer his design in making it. Whatever, in its structure, is adapted to gain that end, we immediately pronounce to be *as it should be*, and whatever obstructs its design, tendency, and operation, we pronounce to be wrong, and to want correction. The same method of judging may be transferred to the works of God; so that whatever it be, in the sentiments or conduct of men, that concurs with, and promotes the design of our maker,

maker, we muſt pronounce to be, therefore, *right*; and whatever tends to thwart
and obſtruct his end, we ought to call
wrong: becauſe, when the former prevails, the great object of the whole ſyſtem is gained; whereas, when the latter
takes place, that end and deſign is defeated.

2. On the other hand, if we were to
form a rule for our conduct independent
of any regard to the divine being, we
ſhould certainly conclude that it is the
part of wiſdom, to provide for our greateſt happineſs; and, conſequently, that we
ſhould cheriſh thoſe ſentiments, and adopt
that conduct, by which it will be beſt ſecured.   But this rule muſt coincide with
the former; becauſe our happineſs is an
object with the divine being no leſs than
it is with ourſelves; for it has been ſhewn,
that benevolence is the ſpring of all his
actions, and that he made us to be happy.

3. Since,

3. Since, however, the divine goodneſs is general, and impartial; and he muſt, conſequently, prefer the happineſs of the *whole,* to that of any *individuals,* it cannot be his pleaſure, that we ſhould conſult our own intereſt, at the expence of that of others. Conſidering ourſelves, therefore, not as ſeparate individuals, but as members of ſociety, another objeſt that we ought to have in view is the welfare of our fellow creatures, and of mankind at large. But ſtill there is no real diſagreement among theſe different rules of conduſt, becauſe we are ſo made, as ſocial beings, that every man provides the moſt effeſtually for his own happineſs, when he cultivates thoſe ſentiments, and purſues that conduſt, which, at the ſame time, moſt eminently conduce to the welfare of thoſe with whom he is conneſted. Such is the wiſdom of this admirable conſtitution, that every individual of the ſyſtem gains his own ends, and thoſe of his maker, by the ſame means.

The

The laſt rule is *conſcience*, which is the reſult of a great variety of impreſſions, the concluſions of our own minds, and the opinions of others, reſpecting what is right and fit in our conduct, forming a ſet of maxims which are ready to be applied upon every emergency, where there would be no time for reaſon or reflecti-on. Conſcience, being a principle thus formed, is properly conſidered as a *ſub-ſtitute* for the three other rules, viz. a regard to the will of God, to our own greateſt happineſs, and the good of others, and it is, in fact, improved and corrected from time to time by having recourſe to theſe rules. This principle of conſcience, therefore, being, as it were, the reſult of all the other principles of our conduct united, muſt deſerve to be conſidered as the guide of life, together with them ; and its dictates, though they vary, in ſome meaſure, with education, and will be found to be, in ſome reſpects, different among different nations of the world, yet, in general, evidently concur in giving
                                                        their

their fanction to the fame rules of conduct, that are fuggefted by the three before mentioned confiderations. For, if
we confider what kind of fentiments and
conduct mankind in general will, without
much reflection, and without hefitation,
pronounce to be right; if we confider
what are the actions that we muft efteem
and admire in others, and that we reflect
upon with the moft fatisfaction in ourfelves, they will appear to be the fame
with thofe which tend to make ourfelves
and others the moft truly happy.

Following thefe four guides, we fhall
find that temperance, or the due government of our paffions, with refpect to ourfelves; juftice, benevolence, and veracity
with refpect to others; together with gratitude, obedience, and refignation to God,
ought to be moft affiduoufly cultivated
by us; as what are, at the fame time, the
moft pleafing to our maker, the moft con-
ducive to our own happinefs, and that of
others, and the moft agreeable to the na-

D   tural

tural and unperverted dictates of conſcience.

That we are capable of governing ourſelves by theſe rules, and, from a proper
regard to motives, can voluntarily chuſe
and purſue that courſe of life which the
will of God, a regard to our own happineſs, to the good of ſociety, and the dictates of our conſciences, uniformly recommend to us, is ſometimes expreſſed
by ſaying that *we are the proper ſubjects of
moral government.* Unleſs we ſuppoſe
that men have this voluntary power over
their actions, whereby they can, at pleaſure, either obey or diſobey the proper
rule of life ; that is, unleſs they be ſo
conſtituted, that the proper motives to
right conduct can have a ſufficient influence upon their minds, all religion is in
vain. To what purpoſe can it be to give
men a law, which it is not in their power to
obſerve ; or what propriety can there be
either in rewarding them for actions to
which they could not contribute, or in
punishing

punifhing them for offences which they could not help. We may, therefore, take it for granted, as the firft, and moft fundamental principle of all religion ; as neceffary to our being the proper fubjects of moral government, that we are equally capable of intending and doing both good and evil ; and therefore that is not in vain that laws are propofed to us, and motives are laid before us, both to perfuade us to what is right, and to diffuade us from what is wrong, fince it depends upon ourfelves, whether we will be influenced by them or not.

If we obferve the proper rules of conduct, or the law of our natures, we fhall fecure to ourfelves many folid advantages ; and if we do not obferve them, we entail upon ourfelves many evils. Thefe are, therefore, called the *punifhments of vice,* and the former the *rewards of virtue* ; and fince they are difpenfed by the providence of God, and take place according to his appointment, in the con-

ftitution

ſtitution of the courſe of nature; he is properly conſidered as our *moral governor*, and *judge*, and we are ſaid to be *accountable* to him for our conduct.

From a regard to the four rules of right and wrong, explained above, I ſhall now endeavour to analize the ſentiments, the paſſions, and affections of mankind, and lay down particular rules for our conduct in life.

S E C T I O N II.

Of the different objects of purſuit, and the different paſſions and affections of men corresponding to them.

IN order to form a proper judgment concerning the conduct of man, as an individual, and a member of ſociety, according to the rules above laid down, it will be neceſſary to have a juſt idea of, and to keep in view, the different objects

of

of our purfuit, and the different paffions and affections of our nature correfponding to them.

We find ourfelves placed in a world, in which we are furrounded by a variety of objects, which are capable of giving us pleafure and pain; and finding by our own experience, and the information of others, in what manner each of them is adapted to affect us, we learn to defire fome of them, and feel an averfion to others. To thefe defires and averfions we give the name of *paffions* or *affections*, and we generally clafs them according to the objects to which they correfpond. Thefe paffions and affections are the fprings of all our actions, and by their means we are engaged in a variety of interefting purfuits through the whole courfe of our lives. When we fucceed in our purfuits, or are in hopes of fucceeding, we are happy; and when we are difappointed in our fchemes, or in fear of being fo, we are unhappy.

D 3 1. The

1. The firſt and loweſt claſs of our deſires is that by which we are prompted to feek after corporeal or fenſual pleaſure, and confequently to avoid bodily pain. Theſe *appetites*, as they are uſually called, to diſtinguiſh them from paſſions of a more refined nature, are common with us and the brutes; and to, all appearance they are poſſeſſed of them in as high a degree as we are, and are capable of receiving as much pleaſure from them as we are. Indeed, the *final cauſe*, or the *objeſt* of theſe appetites is the very ſame with reſpeſt to both, namely, the continuance of life, and the propagation of the ſpecies. It was neceſſary, therefore, that all animals, which have equally their own ſubſiſtence, and the continuance of their ſpecies to provide for, ſhould be equally furniſhed with them.

2. It happens, from a variety of cauſes, that pleaſurable ideas are transferred, by aſſociation, upon objeſts which have not, originally, and in themſelves, the power

of

of gratifying any of our fenfes ;, as thofe which give us the ideas that we call *beautiful* or *fublime*, particularly thofe that occur in works of genius, ftrokes of wit, and in the polite arts of mufic, painting, and poetry. Our capacity for enjoying pleafures of this kind, depending upon the affociation of our ideas, and requiring fuch advances in intellectual life as brutes are incapable of, they are, therefore, claffed under the general denomination of *intellectual pleafures* (a name which we give to all our pleafures, except thofe of fenfe) and more particularly under the head of *pleafures of imagination* ; becaufe the greater part of them are founded on thofe refemblances of things, which are perceived and recollected by that modification of our intellectual powers which we call *fancy*.

3. Another clafs of our paffions may be termed the *focial*, becaufe they arife from our connections with our fellow creatures of mankind; and thefe are of two kinds,

D 4

kinds, conſiſting either in our deſire of
their good opinion, or in our wiſhing their
happineſs or miſery.   In this latter ſpecies
of the claſs, we alſo comprize gratitude
for the favours, and a reſentment of the
wrongs we receive from them.

 Thoſe affections of the mind which reſpect the divine being belong to this claſs,
the object of them being one with whom
we have the moſt intimate connection, to
whom we are under the greateſt obligation, and whoſe approbation is of the
greateſt importance to us.   All the difference there is between our affections, conſidered as having God or man for their
object, ariſes from the difference of their
ſituation with reſpect to us.   The divine
being, ſtanding in no need of our ſervices,
is, therefore, no object of our benevolence, properly ſo called; but the ſentiments of reverence, love, and confidence,
with reſpect to God, are of the ſame nature with thoſe which we exerciſe towards
our fellow creatures, only infinitely exceeding

ceeding them in *degree,* as the divine power, wifdom, and goodnefs, infinitely exceed every thing of the fame kind in man.

Some of the brutes, living in a kind of imperfect fociety, and particularly domeftick animals, are capable of feveral of the paffions belonging to this clafs, as gratitude, love, hatred, &c. but having only a fmall degree of intellect, they are hardly capable of thofe which have for their object the efteem or good opinion of others; which feem to require a confiderable degree of refinement. We fee, however, in horfes, and fome other animals, the ftrongeft emulation, by which they will exert themfelves to the utmoft in their endeavours to furpafs, and overcome others.

4. A fourth fet of paffions is that which has for its object our own *intereft* in general, and is called *felf love.* This feems to require a confiderable degree of refinement, and therefore it is probable that

brute

brute animals have no idea of it. Their chief object is the gratification of their appetites or paſſions, without reflecting upon their *happineſs in general*, or having any ſuch thing in view in their actions.

There is a lower kind of ſelf intereſt, or rather *ſelfiſhneſs*, the object of which is the means of procuring thoſe gratifications to which money can be ſubſervient; and from loving money as a *means* of procuring a variety of pleaſures and conveniences, a man may at length come to purſue it as an *end*, and without any regard to the proper uſe of it. It then becomes a new kind of paſſion, quite diſtinct from any other; inſomuch, that, in order to indulge it, many perſons will deprive themſelves of every natural gratification.

5. Laſtly, as ſoon as we begin to diſtinguiſh among our actions, and are ſenſible that there are reaſons for ſome of them, and againſt others, we get a notion of ſome of them as what *ought* to be performed.

formed, and of others of them as what are, or ought to be refrained from.. In this manner we get the abftract ideas of *right and wrong* in human actions, and a variety of pleafing circumftances attend-ing the former, and difagreeable ones accompanying the latter, we come in time to love fome kinds of actions, and to abhor others, without regard to any other confideration. For the fame reafon certain tempers, or difpofitions of mind, as leading to certain kinds of conduct, become the objects of this moral approbation, or difapprobation; and from the whole, arifes what we call a *moral fenfe,* or a love of virtue and a hatred of vice in the abftract. This is the greateft refinement of which we are capable, and in the due exercife and gratification of it confifts the higheft perfection and happinefs of our natures.

SECTION

SECTION III.

Of the ruling paffion, *and an eftimate of the propriety and value of the different purfuits of mankind.*

HAVING given this general delineation of the various paffions and affections of human nature, which may be called the fprings of all our actions (fince every thing that we do is fomething that we are prompted to by one or more of them,) I fhall now proceed to examine them feparately; in order to afcertain how far we ought to be influenced by any of them, and in what cafes, or degrees, the indulgence of any of them becomes wrong and criminal.

Actuated as we are by a variety of paffions, it can hardly be, but that fome of them will have more influence over us than others. Thefe are fometimes called

ruling

ruling paſſions, becauſe, whenever it happens that the gratification of ſome interferes with that of others, all the reſt will
give place to theſe. If; for inſtance, any
man's ruling paſſion be the love of money,
he will deny himſelf any of the pleaſures
of life for the ſake of it ; whereas,
if the love of pleaſure were his ruling paſſion, he would often run the riſque of
impoveriſhing himſelf, rather than not
procure his favourite indulgence.

It muſt be of great importance, therefore, to know which ought to be our
ruling paſſions through life, or what are
thoſe gratifications and purſuits to which
we ought to ſacrifice every thing elſe.
This is the objeƈt of our preſent inquiry,
in conduƈting which we muſt conſider
how far the indulgence of any particular
paſſion is conſiſtent with our regard to
the four rules of conduƈt that have been
explained; namely, the will of God, our
own beſt intereſt, the good of others, and
the natural diƈtates of our conſcience; and

in

in eſtimating the value of any particular enjoyment, with reſpect to the happineſs we receive from it, we muſt conſider how great or intenſe it is, how long it will continue, whether we regard the nature of the ſenſe from which it is derived, or the opportunities we may have of procuring the gratification of it, and laſtly, how far it is conſiſtent, or inconſiſtent, with other pleaſures of our nature, more or leſs valuable than itſelf.

§ 1. *Of the pleaſures of ſenſe.*

Since no appetite or paſſion belonging to our frame was given us in vain, we may conclude, that there cannot be any thing wrong in the ſimple gratification of *any* deſire that our maker has implanted in us, under certain limitations and in certain circumſtances; and if we conſider the proper object of any of our appetites, or the end it is calculated to anſwer, it will be a rule for us in determining how far the divine being intended that they ſhould be indulged.

indulged. Now fome of our fenfual appetites have for their proper object the
fupport of life, and others the propagation of the fpecies. They fhould, therefore, be indulged as far as is neceffary for
thefe purpofes, and where the indulgence
is not fo exceffive, or fo circumftanced,
as to interfere with the greater good of
ourfelves and others.

1. But to make the gratification of our
fenfes our *primary* purfuit, muft be abfurd; for the appetite for food is given us
for the fake of fupporting life, and not life
for the fake of confuming food. The like
may be faid of other fenfual appetites.
Since, therefore, we certainly err from the
intention of nature when we make that an
end, which was plainly meant to be no more
than a *means* to fome farther end; whatever this great end of life be, we may
conclude that it cannot be the gratification of our fenfual appetites, for they
themfelves are only a means to fomething
elfe.

2. To

2. To make the gratification of our bodily fenfes the chief end of living would tend to defeat itfelf; for a man who fhould have no other end in view would be apt fo to overcharge and furfeit his fenfes, that they would become indifpofed for their proper functions, and indulgence would occafion nothing but a painful loathing. By intemperance alfo in eating and drinking, and in all other corporeal pleafures, the powers of the body itfelf are weakened, and a foundation is laid for diforders the moft loathfome to behold, the moft painful to endure, and the moft fatal in their tendencies and iffues. The ingenuity of man cannot contrive any torture fo exquifite, and at the fame time of fo long continuance, as thofe which are occafioned by the irregular indulgence of the fenfes; whereas temperance, and occafional abftinence, is a means of keeping all the bodily organs and fenfes in their proper tone, difpofed to relifh their proper gratifications; fo that they fhall give a man the moft true

and

and exquifite enjoyment even of fenfual
pleafure. They prolong life to the utmoft term of nature, and contribute to a
peaceful and eafy death.

3. An addictednefs to fenfual pleafure
blunts the faculties of the mind, being
injurious to mental apprehenfion, and all
the finer feelings of the foul, and confequently deprives a man of a great many
fources of pleafures which he might otherwife enjoy, and particularly of that moft
valuable complacency which he might
have in his own difpofitions and conduct;
from a proper and temperate ufe of the
good things of life.

4. Senfual indulgences, though, to a
certain degree, and in certain circumftances, they feem to promote benevolence, are evidently unfriendly to it when
carried beyond that degree; for though
moderate eating and drinking in company
promotes chearfulnefs, and good humour,
excefs frequently gives occafion to quar-
relling

relling and contention, and ſometimes even to murder. Alſo, when a man makes the indulgence of his appetities his primary purſuit, beſides incapacitating himſelf for the ſervice of mankind in any important reſpect, he will ſcruple no means, however baſe, cruel, or unjuſt, to procure himſelf his favourite pleaſures, which he conceives to be in a manner neceſſary to his being.

5. With reſpect to the bulk of mankind, whoſe circumſtances in life are low, the ſole purſuit of ſenſual pleaſure is exceedingly injurious to that induſtry which is neceſſary to their ſupport. Indeed, it is often ſufficient to diſſipate the moſt ample fortune, and reduce men from affluence to poverty, which, in ſuch circumſtances, they are leaſt able to ſtruggle with.

It is impoſſible that we ſhould not condemn a diſpoſition and purſuit ſo circumſtanced as this. An addictedneſs to ſenſual pleaſures is manifeſtly incompatible with our

our own true interest, it is injurious to o-
thers, and, on both thefe accounts, muft
be contrary to the will of God. The
vices of gluttony, drunkennefs, and lewd-
nefs are alfo, clearly contrary to the natural dictates of our minds; and every
man who is guilty of them, feels himfelf
to be defpicable and criminal, both in his
own eyes, and thofe of others.

The only rule with refpect to our *diet*,
is to prefer thofe kinds, and that quantity
of food, which moft conduces to the
health and vigour of our bodies. Whatever in eating or drinking is inconfiftent
with, and obftructs this end, is wrong,
and fhould carefully be avoided; and e-
very man's own experience, affifted with a
little information from others, will be fuf-
ficent to inform him what is nearly the
beft for himfelf in both thofe refpects; fo
that no perfon is likely to injure himfelf
much through mere miftake.

With

With reſpect to thoſe appetites that are ſubſervient to the propagation of the ſpecies, I would obſerve, that the experience of ages teſtifies, that *marriage*, at a proper time of life, whereby one man is confined to one woman, is moſt favourable to health and the true enjoyment of life. It is a means of raiſing the greateſt number of healthy children, and makes the beſt proviſion for their inſtruction and ſettlement in life; and nothing more need be ſaid to ſhew that this ſtate of life has every character of what is right, and what ought to be adopted, in preference to every other mode of indulging our natural paſſions.

Marriage is, moreover, of excellent uſe as a means of transferring our affections from ourſelves to others. We ſee, not in extraordinary caſes, but generally, in common life, that a man even prefers the happineſs of his wife and children to his own; and his regard for them is frequently a motive to ſuch induſtry, and ſuch an
exertion

exertion of his powers, as would make him exceedingly unhappy, if it were not for the confideration of the benefit that accrues to them from it. Nay, in many cafes, we fee men rifking their lives, and even rufhing on certain death, in their defence. The fame, alfo, is generally the attachment of wives to their hufbands, and fometimes, but not fo generally, the attachment of children to their parents.

We may add, that when once a man's affections have been transferred from himfelf to others, even his wife and children, they are more eafily extended to other perfons, ftill more remote from him, and that, by this means, he is in the way of acquiring a principle of general benevolence, patriotifm, and public fpirit, which perfons who live to be old without ever marrying are not fo generally remarkable for. The attention of thefe perfons having been long confined to themfelves, they often grow more and more felfifh and narrow fpirited, fo as to be actuated in all

their

their purfuits by a joylefs defire of accu-
mulating what they cannot confume themfelves, and what they muft leave to thofe
who they know, have but little regard
for them, and for whom they have but
little regard.

A feries of family cafes (in which a
confiderable degree of anxiety and painful fympathy have a good effect) greatly
improves, and as it were *mellows*, the mind
of man. It is a kind of exercife and difcipline, which eminently fits him for great
and generous conduct; and, in fact, makes
him a fuperior kind of being, with refpect
to the generality of thofe who have had
no family connections.

On the other hand, a courfe of lewd
indulgence, without family cafes, finks
a man below his natural level. Promif-
cuous commerce gives an indelible vicious
taint to the imagination, fo that, to the
lateft term of life, thofe ideas will be predominant, which are proper only to
youthful

youthful vigour. And what in nature is more wretched, abfurd, and defpicable; than to have the mind continually haunted with the idea of pleafures which cannot be enjoyed; and which ought to have been long abandoned, for entertainments more fuited to years; and from which, if perfons had been properly trained, they would, in the courfe of nature, have been prepared to receive much greater and fuperior fatisfaction.

Befides, all the pleafures of the fexes in the human fpecies, who cannot fink them-felves fo low as the brutes, depend much upon *opinion,* or particular mental attach-ment; and confequently, they are greatly heightened by fentiments of *love* and *af-fection,* which have no place with common proflitutes, or concubines, where the con-nection is only occafional or temporary, and confequently flight. Thofe perfons, therefore, who give themfelves up to the lawlefs indulgence of their paffions, be-fides being expofed to the moft loathfome

and

and painful diforders, befides exhaufting the powers of nature prematurely, and fubjecting themfelves to fevere remorfe of mind, have not (whatever they may fancy or pretend) any thing like the real pleafure and fatisfaction that perfons generally have in the married ftate.

§ 2. *Of the pleafures of imagination,*

As we ought not to make the gratification of our external fenfes the main end of life, fo neither ought we to indulge our tafte for the more refined pleafures, thofe called the pleafures of imagination, without fome bounds. The cultivation of a tafte for propriety, beauty, and fublimity, in objects natural or artificial, particularly for the pleafures of mufic, painting, and poetry, is very proper in younger life; as it ferves to draw off the attention from grofs animal gratifications, and to bring us a ftep farther into intellectual life; fo as to lay a foundation for higher attainments. But if we ftop here, and devote

our

our whole time, and all our faculties to thefe objects, we fhall certainly fall fhort of the proper end of life.

1. Thefe objects, in general, only give pleafure to a certain degree, and are a fource of more pain than pleafure when a perfon's tafte is arrived to a certain pitch of correctnefs and delicacy: for then hardly any thing will pleafe, but every thing will give difguft that comes not up to fuch an ideal ftandard of perfection as few things in this world ever reach: fo fo that, upon the whole, in this life, at leaft in this country, a perfon whofe tafte is no higher than a *mediocrity* ftands the beft chance for enjoying the pleafures of imagination; and confequently all the time and application that is more than neceffary to acquire this mediocrity of tafte, or excellence in the arts refpecting it, are wholly loft.

Since, however, the perfons and objects with which a man is habitually conver-

E   fant,

fant, are much in his own power, a confiderable refinement of tafte may not,
perhaps, in all cafes, impair the happinefs of life, but, under the direction of
prudence may multiply the pleafures of
it, and give a perfon a more exquifite
enjoyment of it.

2. Very great refinement of tafte, and
great excellence in thofe arts which are
the object of it, are the parents of fuch
exceffive *vanity*, as expofes a man to a
variety of mortifications, and difappoint-
ments in life. They are alfo very apt to
produce envy, jealoufy, peevifhnefs, malice, and other difpofitions of mind, which
are both uneafy to a man's felf, and dif-
qualify him for contributing to the pleafure and happinefs of others. This is
more efpecially the cafe where a man's
excellence lies chiefly in a fingle thing,
which, from confining his attention to it,
will be imagined to be of extraordinary
confequence, while every other kind of
excellence will be undervalued.

3. With

3. With refpect to many perfons, a great refinement of tafte is attended with the fame inconveniences as an addictednefs to fenfual pleafure; for it is apt to lead them into many expences, and make them defpife plain honeft induftry; whereby they are frequently brought into a ftate of poverty, furrounded with a thoufand artificial wants, and without the means of gratifying them.

A tafte for the pleafures of imagination ought, more particularly, to be indulged, and even encouraged, in younger life, in the interval between a ftate of mere animal nature, in a child, and the ferious purfuits of manhood. It is alfo a means of relaxing the mind from too clofe an attention to ferious bufinefs, through the whole of life, promoting innocent amufement, chearfulnefs, and good humour. Befides, a tafte for natural, and alfo for artificial propriety, beauty, and fublimity, has a connection with a tafte for moral propriety, moral beauty, and dignity;

E 2 and

and when properly cultivated, enables u:
to take more pleaſure in the contempla
tioń of the works, perfeƈtions, and pro
vidence of God. Here, indeed, it is, thaɩ
a juſt taſte for theſe refined pleaſures findſ
its higheſt and moſt perfeƈt gratification
for it is in theſe contemplations, that inſtances of the moſt exquiſite propriety,
beauty, and grandeur occur.

§ 3. *Of ſelf intereſt.*

A regard to our greateſt happineſs waʂ
allowed before to be one of the propeɩ
rules of our conduƈt; but at the ſame timɩ
it was ſhewn to be only one of four; anɗ
in faƈt the proper end of it, or our greateſɩ
happineſs as individuals, is moſt effeƈtu
ally gained, when it is not itſelf the im
mediate ſcope of our aƈtions; that is,
when we have not our intereſt direƈtly iɩ
view, but when we are aƈtuated by ɑ
diſintereſted regard to the good of others,
to the commands of God, and to the dictates of conſcience.

1. Wh'"

1. When we keep up a regard to ourselves in our conduct, we can never exclude such a degree of anxiety, and jealousy of others, as will always make us in some degree unhappy; and we find by experience, that no persons have so true and unallayed enjoyments, as those who lose sight of themselves, and of all regard to their own happiness, in higher and greater pursuits.

2. Though it be true, that, when our interest is perfectly understood, it will be found to be best promoted by those actions which are dictated by a regard to the good of others, &c. it requires great comprehension of mind even to see this, and much more to act upon it; so that if the bulk of mankind were taught to pursue their own proper happiness, as the *ultimate end* of life, they would be led to do many things injurious to others, not being able to see how they could otherwise make the best provision for themselves.

P 5   E 3   3. If

3. If we conſult the unperverted dictates of our minds, we ſhall feel that there is a kind of *meanneſs* in a man's acting from a view to his own intereſt only; and if any perſon were known to have no higher motive for his conduct, though he ſhould have ſo much comprehenſion of mind, as that this principle ſhould never miſlead him, and every particular action which he was led to by it ſhould be, in itſelf, always right, he would not be allowed to have any *moral worth*, ſo as to command our *eſteem*; and he would not at all engage our *love*. All we could ſay in his favour would be that he was a *prudent* man, not that he was *virtuous*. Nay we ſhould not allow that any man's conduct was even *right*, in the higheſt and moſt proper ſenſe of the word, unleſs he was influenced by motives of a higher and purer nature; namely, a regard to the will of God, to the good of others, or to the dictates of conſcience.

It

It seems to follow from these considerations, that this principle, of a regard to our higheſt intereſt, holds a kind of *middle rank* between the vices and the virtues ; and that its principal uſe is to be a means of raiſing us above all the lower and vicious purſuits, to thoſe that are higher, and properly ſpeaking virtuous and praiſe worthy. From a regard to our true intereſt, or mere ſelf love, we are firſt of all made ſenſible that we ſhould injure ourſelves by making the gratification of our ſenſes, or the pleaſures of imagination, &c. our chief purſuit, and the great buſineſs and end of life ; and we are convinced that it is our wiſdom to pay a ſupreme regard to the will of our maker, to employ ourſelves in doing good to others, and, univerſally, to obey the dictates of our conſciences ; and this perſuaſion will lead us to do thoſe things which we know to be agreeable to thoſe higher principles, though we cannot immediately ſee them to be for our intereſt ; and, by degrees, we ſhall get a habit of acting in the moſt

' pious,

pious, generous, and conſcientious manner, without ever having our own happineſs in view, or in the leaſt attending to
any connection, immediate or diſtant, that
our conduct has with it.

On theſe accounts, it ſeems better not
to conſider any kind of ſelf intereſt as an
ultimate rule of our conduct; but that,
independent of any regard to our own
happineſs, we ſhould think ourſelves o-
bliged conſcientiouſly to do what is right,
and generouſly and diſintereſtedly to pur--
ſue the good of others, though, to all appearance, we ſacrifice our own to it; and at
all events to conform to the will of our
maker, who, ſtanding in an equal relation
to all his offspring, muſt wiſh the good
of them all, and therefore cannot approve of our conſulting our own happineſs at the expence of that of others, but
muſt rather take pleaſure in ſeeing us act
upon the maxims of his own generous benevolence; depending, in general, that
that great, righteous, and good being,
who

who approves of our conduct, will not suffer us to be lofers by it upon the whole.

There is a lower fpecies of felf intereft, or *felfifhnefs*, confifting in the *love of money*, which, beyond a certain degree, is highly deferving of cenfure. As a means of procuring ourfelves any kind of gratification, that can be purchafed, the love of money is a paffion of the fame nature with a fondnefs for that fpecies of pleafure that can be purchafed with it. If, for inftance, a man makes no other ufe of his wealth than to procure the means of fenfual pleafure, the love of money, in him, is only another name for the love of pleafure. If a man accumulates money with no other view than to indulge his tafte in the refined arts above mentioned, his love of money is the fame thing with a love of the arts; or laftly if a man really intends nothing but the good of others while he is amaffing riches, he is actuated by the principle of benevolence. In fhort, the love of money, whenever it is purfued,

directly

directly and properly, as *a means* to ſomething elſe, is a paſſion, the rank of which
keeps pace with the *end* that is propoſed
to be gained by it. But in the purſuit of
riches, it is very common to forget the
uſe of money as a means; and to deſire
it without any farther end, ſo as even to
ſacrifice to this purſuit all thoſe appetites
and paſſions, to the gratification of which
it was originally ſubſervient, and for the
ſake of which only it was originally covet-
ed. In this ſtate the love of money, or
the paſſion we call *covetouſneſs*, is evidently abſurd and wrong.

This groſs ſelf intereſt, which conſiſts
in an exceſſive love of money, as an end,
and without any regard to its uſe, will
ſometimes bring a man to abridge himſelf
of all the natural enjoyments of life, and
engage him in the moſt laborious purſuits,
attended with moſt painful anxiety of
mind; it very often ſteels his heart againſt
all the feelings of humanity and compaſ-
ſion, and never fails to fill him with envy,
jealouſy,

jealoufy, and refentment againft all thofe whom he imagines to be his competitors and rivals. Much lefs does this fordid paffion admit of any of the pleafures that refult from a confcioufnefs of the appro- bation of God, of our fellow creatures, or of our own minds, In fact, it deprives a man of all the genuine pleafures of his nature, and involves him in much per- plexity and diftrefs ; the immediate caufe of which, though it be often abfurd and imaginary, is ferious to himfelf, and makes him appear in a ridiculous light to others.

All thefe obfervations, concerning the love of money, are equally true of the love of *power*, or of any thing elfe, that is originally defirable as a *means* to fome farther end, but which afterwards be- comes itfelf an ultimate end of our ac- tions. It is even, in a great meafure, true of the love of *knowledge* or *learning.* This is chiefly ufeful as a means, and is valuable in proportion to the end it is fit-

ted.

ted to anfwer; but, together with the love of riches, and power, it is abfurd, and to be condemned, when purfued as an end, or for its own fake only.

The amaffing of money muft be allowed to be reafonable, or at leaft *excufable*, provided there be a probability that a man may live to enjoy it, or that it may be of ufe to his pofterity, or others in whofe welfare he interefts himfelf; but when we fee a man perfifting in the accumulation of wealth, even to extreme old age, when it would be deemed madnefs in him to pretend that he could have any real want of it; when he difcovers the fame avaricious temper though he has no children, and there is no body for whom he is known to have the leaft regard, it is evident that he purfues money as an *end*, or for *its own fake*, and not at all as a *means* to any thing farther. In this cafe, therefore, it is, without doubt, highly criminal, and deferving of the above mentioned cenfures.

§ 4. *Of*

§ 4. *Of the paſſions which ariſe from our
ſocial nature.*

The paſſions and affections which I
have hitherto conſidered are thoſe which
belong to us as individuals, and do not
neceſſarily ſuppoſe any relation to other
beings, I ſhall now proceed to treat of
thoſe which are of this latter claſs, and firſt
of the pleaſure that we take in the good
opinion of others concerning us, which
gives riſe to that paſſion which we call the
love of fame.

This is a paſſion that diſcovers itſelf
pretty early in life, and ariſes principally
from our experience and obſervation of
the many advantages that reſult from the
good opinion of others. In the early
part of life this principle is of ſignal uſe
to us, as a powerful incentive to thoſe actions which procure us the eſteem of our
fellow creatures ; which are, in general,
the ſame that are dictated by the princi-

ples

ples of benevolence and the moral ſenſe, and alſo by a regard to the will of God.

  But though, by this account, the love of fame is an uſeful *ally* to virtue, the gratification of it ought by no means to be made our primary purſuit; becauſe, if it were known that *fame* was the ſole end of a man's actions, he would be ſo far from gaining this end, that he would be deſpiſed by mankind in general; and eſpecially if he were advanced in life, when it is commonly expected that men ſhould be governed by higher and better principles. For no actions are looked upon by the bulk of mankind as properly praiſe worthy, but thoſe which proceed from a principle of diſintereſted benevolence, obedience to God, or a regard to conſcience.

  2. Beſides, *humility* is a principal ſubject of praiſe; and, indeed, without this, no other virtue is held in much eſteem. Now this humility ſuppoſes ſuch a diffidence of ones ſelf, ſuch a readineſs to ac
knowledge

knowledge the fuperiority of others, and alfo fo fmall a degree of complacence in the contemplation of our own excellencies, as muſt be inconſiſtent with our making this pleaſure our chief purſuit, and the ſource of our greateſt happineſs.

3. In another reſpect, alfo, the love of fame, as a primary object of purſuit, tends to defeat itſelf. We are not pleaſed with praiſe, except it come from perſons of whoſe *judgment*, as well as *ſincerity* we have a good opinion ; but the love of fame, as our ſupreme good, tends to beget ſuch a degree of *ſelf ſufficiency*, and conceit, as makes us deſpiſe the reſt of mankind, that is, it makes their praiſe of little value to us ; fo that the ſprightly pleaſures of *vanity* naturally give place in time to all the ſullenneſs and moroſeneſs of *pride*.

4. If a man have no other object than reputation or popularity, he will be led to dwell frequently upon the ſubject of

his

his own merit, of which he will, confequently, entertain an overweening and un-
reaſonable opinion; and this can hardly
fail to produce, beſides a moſt ridiculous
degree of conceit, ſo much envy and jealouſy, as will make him inſufferable in ſociety, and ſubject him to the moſt cutting
mortifications.

5. If a man's principal object be thoſe
qualifications and actions which uſually
diſtinguiſh men, and make them much
talked of, both in their own and future
ages, ſuch as eminence with reſpect to
genius, excellence in the polite arts, diſ-
coveries in ſcience, or great achivements
in the arts of peace or war, his chance of
ſucceeding is very ſmall; for it is not poſſible that more than a *few* perſons, in com-
pariſon, can draw the attention of the
reſt of mankind upon them. And beſides that the qualifications which are the
foundation of this eminence are very rare
among mankind, ſuccefs depends upon
the concurrence of many *circumſtances,*

independent

independent on a man's felf. It is plain, therefore, that very few perfons can reafonably hope to diftinguifh themfelves in this manner, and it would certainly be very wrong to propofe that as a principal object of purfuit to all mankind, which the bulk of them cannot poffibly obtain, or enjoy.

The proper ufe of this love of fame, as of the principle of felf intereft, is to be a means of bringing us within the influence of better and truly virtuous principles, in confequence of begetting a habit of doing the fame things which better principles would prompt to. If, for inftance, a man fhould, firft of all, perform acts of charity and beneficence from oftentation only, the joy that he actually communicates to others, and the praifes he receives for his generofity, from thofe who are ftrangers to his real motive, cannot but give him an idea of the purer pleafures of genuine benevolence, from which, and not from a defire of applaufe only, he will for the future act. The

The pleaſures that accrue to us from the purſuit of fame, like thoſe of ſelf intereſt, are beſt gained by perſons who have them not directly in view. The man who is truly benevolent, pious, and conſcientious, will, in general, ſecure the moſt ſolid and permanent reputation with mankind; and if he be ſo ſituated that the practice of any real virtue ſhall be deemed unfaſhionable, and ſubject him to contempt and inſult, he will have acquired that *ſuperiority of mind*, which will ſet him above it; ſo that he will not feel any pain from the want of ſuch eſteem, as muſt have been purchaſed by the violation, or neglect of his duty. But he will rather applaud himſelf, and rejoice that he is not eſteemed by perſons of certain characters, be they ever ſo numerous, and diſtinguiſhed on certain accounts; finding more than an equivalent recompence in the approbation of his own mind, in the eſteem of the wiſe and good, though they be ever ſo few, and eſpecially in the favour of God, who is the ſearcher of hearts,

hearts, the beft judge, and moft munifici-
ent rewarder of real worth.

§ 5. *Of the fympathetic affections.*

A paffion for fame, though it be founded on the relation that men ftand in to one
another, and therefore fuppofes fociety,
is of a very different nature from the *focial
principle*, properly fo called ; or a difpofition to love, and to do kind offices to
our fellow creatures.

1. That it is with the greateft juftice
that this is ranked among our higheft purfuits has been fhewn already. That the
ftudy to do good to others, is placed in
this rank muft be perfectly agreeable
to the will of God, who cannot but in-
tend the happinefs of all his offspring,
and who is himfelf actuated by the principle of univerfal benevolence. If we
confult the natural dictates of our confcience, we fhall find that it gives the
ftrongeft approbation to difinterefted benevolence

nevolence in ourſelves or others; and if
we examine how our own higheſt intereſt
is affected by it; we ſhall find that, in
general, the more exalted is our benevolence, and the more we lay ourſelves out
to promote the good of others, the more
perfect enjoyment we have of ourſelves,
and the more we are in the way of receiving good offices from others in return;
and, upon the whole, the happier we are
likely to be.

2. A man of a truly benevolent diſpoſition, and who makes the good of others
the object of his purſuit, will never want
opportunities of employing and gratifying
himſelf: for we are ſo connected with
and dependent upon one another, the
ſmall upon the great, and the great upon
the ſmall, that, whatever be a man's ſta-
tion in life, if he be of a benevolent diſpoſition, it will always be in his power to
oblige others, and thereby indulge himſelf.

3. A

3. A person so benevolent may, in general, depend upon success in his schemes, because mankind are previously disposed to approve, recommend, and countenance benevolent undertakings; and though such a person will see much misery and distress, which he cannot relieve, and which will, consequently, give him some pain; yet, upon the whole, his pleasures will he far superior to it; and the pains of sympathy do not, in general, agitate the mind beyond the limits of pleasure. We have even a kind of satisfaction with ourselves in contemplating scenes of distress, though we can only *wish* to relieve the unhappy sufferers. For this reason it is that tragic scenes, and tragical stories are so engaging. This kind of satisfaction has even more charms for mankind in general than the view of many pleasing scenes of life.

4. Besides if to the principle of benevolence be added a strict regard to conscience, and confidence in divine providence, all the pains of sympathy will almost wholly

wholly vaniſh. If we are conſcious that we do all we can to aſſiſt and relieve others, we may have perfect ſatisfaction in ourſelves, and may habitually rejoice in the belief of the wiſdom and goodneſs of God; being convinced that all the evils, which we ineffectually ſtrive to remove, are appointed for wiſe and good purpoſes; and that, being of a temporary nature, they will finally be abſorbed in that infinity of happineſs, to which, though in ways unknown to us, we believe them to be ſubſervient.

Every argument by which benevolence is recommended to us condemns *malevolence,* or a diſpoſition to rejoice in the miſery, and to grieve at the happineſs of others. This baleful diſpoſition may be generated by frequently conſidering our own intereſt as in oppoſition to that of others. For, in this caſe, at the ſame time that we receive pleaſure from our own gain, we receive pleaſure alſo from their loſs, which is connected with it; and for the ſame reaſon, when we grieve for our

own

own lofs, we grieve at their gain. In this manner emulation, envy, jealoufy, and at length actual hatred, and malice, are produced in our hearts.

It is for this reafon that *gaming* is unfavourable to benevolence, as well as other virtues, and high gaming exceedingly pernicious. For, in this cafe, every man's gain is directly produced by another's lofs; fo that the gratification of the one and the difappointment of the other muft always go together. Indeed, upon the fame juft principle, all trade and commerce, all buying and felling, is wrong, unlefs it be to the advantage of both parties.

Malevolent difpofitions, befides that they are clearly contrary to the will of God, and the dictates of confcience, are the fource of much pain and mifery to ourfelves. They confift of very uneafy feelings; fo that no man can be happy, or enjoy any fatisfaction, while he is under the influence of them. Even the pleafures pleaſures of revenge are ſhocking to think of, and what a man muſt deſpiſe himſelf for being capable of reliſhing and enjoying; and, they are, in all caſes, infinitely inferior to the noble ſatisfaction which a man feels in forgiving an injury. There is a meanneſs in the former, but true greatneſs of mind, and real dignity in the latter, and the pleaſure which it gives does not pall upon reflection. Beſides, a diſpoſition to do ill offices to others expoſes a man to the hatred and ill offices of others. The malevolent man arms all mankind againſt him.

Anger, indeed, is in ſome caſes, reaſonable; as when it is directed againſt the vicious, and injurious, who are the peſts of ſociety; ſo that being enemies to ſuch perſons is being friends to mankind at large. But here great caution ſhould be uſed, left this paſſion of anger ſhould, as it is very capable of doing, degenerate into pure ill will towards thoſe who are the objects of it. Nay we ſhould never indulge

dulge to anger fo far as to ceafe to have the real good and welfare of the offender at heart, but be ready even to do our greateft perfonal enemies any kind office in our power, provided that the confequence of it would not be injurious to fociety. This, indeed, is what the law of univerfal benevolence plainly requires, as it ftrictly forbids the doing any *unneceffary* evil; and that evil is unneceffary, which the good and happinefs of others does not require. If, therefore, we would appear to act upon this principle, we muft be careful fo to conduct our refentment, that it may be manifeft, that it is with reluctance that we entertain fentiments of enmity.

If it be our duty to bear good will even to our enemies, much more fhould we exercife it to our real friends, and ufe our endeavours to make the moft ample return for any kindnefs that they do to us. Indeed there is no virtue which has a ftronger teftimony in the confciences of all men,

than

than *gratitude*, and no vice is universally fo hateful as ingratitude.

If the good of fociety be our object, there can be no queftion, but that *veracity*, with refpect to all our declarations, and *fidelity*, with refpect to all our engagements, is one of the moft important of all focial duties. All the purpofes of fociety would be defeated, if falfehood were as common as truth among mankind; and in thofe circumftances all beneficial intercourfe would foon ceafe among them; and, notwithftanding temporary inconveniences may fometimes arife from a rigid adherence to truth, they are infinitely overbalanced by the many fuperior advantages that arife from our depending upon the regard to it being inviolable.

Since an *oath*, or an appeal to divine being, is the moft deliberate, and the moft folemn of all the modes of affeveration, it ought to be the moft fcrupuloufly obferved. There is not, in the nature of things,

things, any ſtronger guard againſt impoſition and deceit, and therefore a perſon who has once *perjured* himſelf, deſerves not only to be deteſted, and ſhunned, as the bane of ſociety, but to be expelled out of it.

§ 5. *Of the relative duties.*

As we ſtand in a variety of relations to one another, and have much more opportunity of doing kind offices to ſome than to others, we cannot ſuppoſe that the divine being intended that our benevolence ſhould be like his own, *univerſal* and *impartial.* He ſtands in the ſame relation to all his creatures, and he is capable of attending to the wants of them all; whereas our beneficence is neceſſarily limited, and therefore ſhould flow the moſt freely towards thoſe whom we can moſt conveniently and effectually ſerve. Beſides the good of the whole will be beſt provided for by every perſon making this a rule to himſelf; whereas, if every per-

ſon,

ſon, without any particular regard to his own limited province, ſhould extend his care to the wants of mankind in general, very little good would, in fact, be done by any.

The *domeſtic relations* of life are the foundation of the ſtrongeſt claim upon our benevolence and kindneſs. The intereſts of *huſband and wife* are the ſame, and inſeparable, and they muſt neceſſarily paſs a very great part of their time together. In theſe circumſtances, to be mutually happy, their affection muſt be ſtrong and undivided. The welfare of their offspring, likewiſe, requires this, that they may give their united care and attention to form their bodies and minds, in order to fit them for the buſineſs of life, and to introduce them with advantage into the world.

As nature makes children the charge of their parents in younger life, ſo it lays an equal obligation on children to provide for their parents, when they are old and infirm,

infirm, and unable to provide for themfelves.

Mafters and fervants are under a variety
of mutual obligations ; and if that connection be happy, and mutually advantageous, there mult be juftice, humanity,
and liberality on the one hand, requited
with fidelity, reafonable fubmiffion, and
affection on the other.

Our own country, likewife, claims a
particular preference. We ought to give
more attention to its welfare than to that
of any other country, and its magiftrates
are intitled to our particular reverence and
refpect.

It is for the good of the whole that we
proportion our regards and benevolent attention in this manner, that is, regulating
them, according to thofe connections in
life that are of the moft importance to our
own happinefs ; but ftill, we fhould never
lofe fight of the relation we ftand in to

F 3   all

all mankind, and all the creation of God ;
with reſpect to whom we are brethren, and
fellow ſubjects ; and whenever the intereſt of ourſelves, our own families, or
country does not greatly interfere, we
ſhould lay ourſelves out to do good to
ſtrangers and foreigners, or to any perſons
that may ſtand in need of our aſſiſtance ;
doing to others as we would they ſhould
do to us ; which is a rule of the goſpel
that is perfectly agreeable to natural
reaſon.

§ 6. *Of the Theopathetic affections.*

As benevolence, or the love of mankind, ſo alſo the love of God, and de-
votedneſs to him bears every character of
one of our higheſt and moſt proper principles of conduct.

1. This principle interferes with no
real gratification, but in ſuch a manner
that all the reſtraint it lays upon any of
them is, in reality, favourable to the true
and

and perfect enjoyment we derive from them. No pains that we can expofe our-felves to for the fake of mortifying our-felves, can be pleafing to that being who made us to be happy, and who has, for that purpofe, given us the power and the means of a variety of gratifications, fuit-ed to our ftate and condition. In this ge-neral manner it is fhewn that the love of God, and devotednefs to him, is perfectly agreeable to a regard to our own greateft good. This principle muft be confiftent with our attention to the good of others, becaufe God is the father of us all, and we are equally his offspring; and nature teaches us to confider him as our father, moral governor, and judge, and therefore to reverence, love, and obey him without referve.

2. An intire devotednefs to God, faith in his providence, and refignation to his will, is the beft antidote againft all the evils of life. If we firmly believe that nothing comes to pafs, refpecting our-

F 4   felves,

ſelves, our friends, and our deareſt intereſts, but by his appointment or permiſ-
ſion; and that he appoints or permits
nothing but for the beſt purpoſes, we ſhall
not only *acquieſce,* but *rejoice* in all the e-
vents of life, proſperous or adverſe. We
ſhall conſider every thing as a means to a
great, glorious, and joyful end; the conſideration of which will reflect a luſtre
upon every thing that leads to it, that has
any connection with it, or the moſt dif-
tant reference to it.

3. Other affections may not always
find their proper gratification, and therefore may be the occaſion of *pain* as well as
of *pleaſure* to us. Even the moſt benevolent purpoſes are frequently diſappointed,
and without faith in the providence of
God, who has the good of all his offspring
at heart, would be a ſource of much ſor-
row and diſquiet to us. But the man
whoſe ſupreme delight ariſes from the
ſenſe of his relation to his maker, from
contemplating his perfections, his works,
- and

and his providence; and who has no will but his, muſt be poſſeſſed of a never failing ſource of joy and ſatisfaction. Every object that occurs to a perſon of this diſpoſition will be viewed in the moſt favourable light; and whether it be immediately, pleaſurable or painful, the relation it bears to God, and his moral government, will make it welcome to him.

4. If we conſider the foundation of the duty and affection we owe to God upon the natural principles of right and equity, in the ſame manner as, from the ſame natural dictates, we judge of the duty we owe to mankind, we cannot but readily conclude, that, if a *human* father, benefactor, governor, and judge, is intitled to our love, reverence, and obedience; he who is, in a much higher and a more perfect ſenſe, our father, benefactor, governor, and judge, muſt be intitled to a greater portion of our love, reverence, and obedience; becauſe, in all theſe relations, he has done, and is continually do-

F 5 ing

ing more to deſerve them. Conſidering
what we have received, and what we daily
receive from God, even life and all the
powers and enjoyments of it; conſidering
our preſent privileges, and our future
hopes, it is impoſſible that our attention,
attachment, ſubmiſſion, and confidence,
ſhould exceed what is reaſonable and properly due to him.

In the regulation of our devotion, we
ſhould carefully avoid both *enthuſiaſm* and
ſuperſtition, as they both ariſe from unworthy notions of God, and his moral
government. The former conſiſts in a
childiſh fondneſs, familiarity, and warmth
of paſſion, and an aptneſs, on that account, to imagine that we are the peculiar favourites of the divine being, who is
the father, friend, and moral governor of
all his creatures. Beſides this violent affection cannot, in its own nature, be of
long continuance. It will, of courſe, a-
bate of its fervour; and thoſe who have
given way to it will be apt to think of
God

God with the other extreme of coldnefs
and indifference; the confequence of which
is often extreme dejection, fear, anxiety,
and diftruft; and fometimes it ends in defpair, and impiety.

On the other hand, *fuperftition* arifes
from miftaking the proper object of the
divine favour and approbation, for want
of having a juft idea of the moral perfections of God, and of the importance of
real virtue. Perfons of this character are
extremely punctual with refpect to the
means and *circumftantials* of religion, or
things that have only an imaginary relation to it, and may be quite foreign to
its real nature; inftead of bringing to
God the devotion of the heart, and the
proper fruits of it, in the faithful difcharge of the duties of life, in the perfonal and focial capacities. The omiffion
of fome mere form, or ceremony, fhall
give fuch perfons more real uneafinefs than
the neglect of a moral duty; and when
they have complied with all the forms

which

which they think requiſite to be obſerved, their conſciences are intirely eaſy, their former guilt has no preſſure, and they are ready to contract new debts, to be wiped off in the ſame manner Almoſt all the religion of the Mahometans and Papiſts conſiſts in this kind of ſuperſtition, and there is too much of it in all ſects and de-nominations of chriſtians. I cannot give a clearer idea of the nature of ſuperſtition than by what appeared in the conduct of ſome Roman Catholicks in Ireland, who, I have been told, broke into a houſe, where they were guilty of robbery and murder, but, ſitting down to regale them-ſelves, would not taſte fleſh meat, becauſe it was Friday.

There is no quality of the heart ſo va-luable as a juſt and manly piety, and no-thing ſo abject and pernicious as ſuperſti-tion. Superſtition and enthuſiaſm are ge-nerally denominated the two *extremes* of religion, and in ſome ſenſes they are ſo; but, at the ſame time, they have a near connection.

connection with one another, and nothing is more common than for perfons to pafs from the one to the other, or to live under the alternate, or even the conftant influence of them both, without entertaining one fentiment of generous and ufeful devotion. Indeed the ufual ground of the prefumption and rapture of the enthufiaft is fome external obfervance, or internal feeling, that can have no claim to the folid approbation of a reafonable being.

§ 7. *Of the obligation of confcience.*

In order to govern our conduct by a regard to our true intereft, to the good of mankind, or the will of God, it is neceffary that we ufe our reafon, that we *think* and *reflect* before we act. Another principle, therefore, was neceffary, to dictate to us on fudden *emergencies,* and to prompt us to right action *without reafoning* or thinking at all. This principle we call *confcience,* and being the natural

fub-

ſubſtitute of all the three other rules of right conduct, it muſt have the ſame title to our regard. As this principle, how‧ ever, is a thing of a variable nature, it muſt be corrected from time to time, by recurring to the principles out of which it was formed. Otherwiſe, as we ſee exemplified in fact, conſcience may come to dictate things moſt injurious to our own good, or that of others, and even moſt diſhonourable to God. What impurities, what ridiculous penances and mortifications, yea what villainies and cruelties do we not find to have been acted by mankind, under the notion of rendering themſelves acceptable to the object of their ſupreme worſhip. - -

If, however, a perſon has been well educated in a chriſtian and proteſtant country, and has lived ſome time under the influence of good impreſſions, ſuch as are favourable to virtue and happineſs, the dictates of his conſcience (which has been formed from thoſe good principles) ‧ will

will generally be right, and may be depended upon not to miflead him. At all events, it is very dangerous to flight and difregard the real dictates of our own minds, fo as either to do what we have a feeling of as wrong, and what we condemn ourfelves for at the time, or to forbear to do what appears to us to be right, what we ought to do, and what we feel a fudden impulfe to do. For if we can difregard even an *erroneous confcience* we may come to difregard the authority of *confcience in general*, and *as fuch*, which after all, is the fureft and beft guardian of our virtue.

2. If the principle of confcience has been well formed, in confequence of a juft train of fentiments, and proper impreffions, fince it is the refult of rational felf intereft, benevolence, and piety, jointly, it may be confidered as the very quinteffence and perfection of our rational natures; fo that to do a thing becaufe it is *right*, will be to act from a nobler, and

more

more exalted principle of conduct, than any of the others. For it is, in fact, every juſt principle united, and reduced into one; and, on this account, it will natu- rally claim the preheminence over the dic- tates of any of them ſingly, ſuppoſing them to claſh; and many caſes may be put, in which it ought to correct and over rule any of them.

The regard I have to my own intereſt, believing it to be my higheſt, the love I bear to my fellow creatures, or even what I take to be the command of God, may dictate one thing, when my ſenſe of right and wrong, whether natural or acquired, may dictate another; and it may be ſafeſt and beſt for me to follow this guide. Thus a papiſt may really believe that he does good to the ſouls, by tormenting the bodies of his fellow creatures, and thereby does God ſervice, and that it is no ſin to deceive hereticks; but if he feel an in- ward reluctance in purſuing perſecuting meaſures, and cannot tell a deliberate falſhood

falſhood without compunction, we ſhould not heſitate to pronounce, that he would do well to forbear that conduct, notwith-ſtanding his belief that he is thereby con-ſulting the good of mankind, and the glory of God; at leaſt till he hath care-fully compared the dictates of his conſci-ence with what he imagined to be the command of God.

3. The ſatisfaction that reſults from obey-ing the dictates of conſcience is of a ſolid and permanent kind, and affords conſola-tion under all the pains and troubles of life. Whatever befall a man, if he can ſay that he hath done his *duty*, and can believe himſelf, he will not be wholly un-happy. On the other hand, the pangs of a guilty conſcience are the moſt intole-rable of all evils. One villainous action is ſufficient to imbitter a man's whole life, and years of remorſe will not make the reflection upon it leſs cutting and diſquiet-ing. All the riches, honours, and luxury of life are not ſufficient to give eaſe to the

mind

mind of that man, who thoroughly con-, demns and abhors himſelf.

4. This mechanical and neceſſary deter-·mination in favour of ſome actions, and againſt others, being either connate with the mind, or, which comes to the ſame thing, ariſing neceſſarily from our conſti-tution, as influenced by the circumſtances of our being, muſt have been intended for ſome very important purpoſe; and this, in its own nature, can be no other than to be the monitor and guide of life. It is, in a manner, felt to be the repreſenta-tive of God himſelf, and therefore, its ſentence will be conſidered as the forerun-ner of the righteous ſentence which our maker and ſovereign judge will paſs upon us. It is not only preſent pain that diſ-quiets the guilty mind, but a dread of fu-ture and divine judgments; as, on the other hand, the approbation of our own hearts is the moſt pleaſing feeling a man can have, not on its own account, ſo much as its being a kind of certificate of the di-vine

vine approbation, and a foretaſte of his future favour and reward.

SECTION IV.

Of the means of virtue.

HAVING thus ſhown the rank and value of all our paſſions and affections, or the regard that is due to each in the conduct of our lives. I ſhall give ſome practical directions, how to ſuppreſs what is irregular and vicious, and promote what is right and virtuous in us.

1. If any of our inferior paſſions have gained the aſcendency in us, ſo that a propenſity to any ſpecies of indulgence is become exceſſive, and, in conſequence of it, bad habits have been formed, it is
certainly

certainly a man's wiſdom, as ſoon as he
begins to ſuſpeƈt that he is in a wrong
courſe, to weigh in his own mind ſuch
conſiderations as have been mentioned
above, reſpecting the nature and tendency
of our paſſions ; that he may thoroughly
convince himſelf how fooliſh a part he has
choſen for himſelf, how injurious his conduƈt is to others, how diſpleaſing to his
maker, and how much it is the cauſe of
ſhame and remorſe to himſelf. It is generally through want of timely *refleƈtion*,
that men abandon themſelves to irregular
indulgences, and contraƈt bad habits ;
ſo that if they would give themſelves time
to *think*, and conſider deliberately of the
nature and conſequences of their conduƈt,
they would chuſe a wiſe and virtuous
courſe. For no man is ſo infatuated as,
that, when no particular temptation is
preſent, when he is perfectly maſter of
himſelf, and cannot but ſee what is for
his true intereſt, purpoſely and knowingly
to lay aſide all regard to it. All mankind wiſh to be happy, and no man can
voluntarily

voluntarily chuse to be miserable. Were any man, therefore, truly sensible, that there is no kind of vice to which he does not sacrifice either the health of his body, his reputation with the thinking part of mankind, or even his worldly interest, sometimes all these together, and always the peace and tranquillity of his mind, who would chuse to persist in it; admitting that a regard to the good of others, and to the known will of God should have no weight among them; though there are few persons, I believe, who are not more or less influenced even by these generous and disinterested considerations.

2. Particular care should be taken on our entrance into the world, that we contract no bad habits; for such is the nature of habits, that when once a man has been accustomed to any thing, it may give him the greatest pain to break himself of it, even though he have no pleasure, yea though he be really unhappy in continuing in it. Youth is, on every account, that

time

time of life which requires our greateſt attention, for then only is the mind ſuſceptible of new impreſſions, ſo as to be capable of changing for the better. When once a man's connections and mode of life have been ſettled, which is generally before, or ſoon after he is arrived at thirty years of age, the bent of his mind is compleatly formed, and it is a thouſand to one but that after this there will be no material change in his diſpoſition or conduct to the end of his life. If his mind be vitiated then, there is little hope of a change, without a total revolution in his connections and affairs ; or unleſs his mind be rouſed by ſome uncommon calamity. In this caſe, entering, as it were, upon life again, with wiſdom bought by experience, his old connections being broken, and new ones to be formed, he may chuſe a wiſer courſe, and in time may make it familiar and pleaſing to him. But ſtill there is great danger of his relapſing into his former habits, the firſt opportunity.

A new

A new fet of *principles*, new *views* and *expectations* may be equivalent to fuch an intire revolution in a man's affairs as was mentioned above. For many perfons are fo difpofed that if they had more *know-ledge* they would have more *virtue*. Thus the doctrines of a refurrection, and of a future ftate of retribution, produced a very great and fpeedy change in the moral ftate of the heathen world, at the firft promulgation of chriftianity, affecting the old as well as the young. But when nothing *new* takes place, with refpect either to a man's circumftances, or his knowledge, there is but little probability that his conduct will be materially affected by an attention to *truths* and *facts*, to the contemplation of which he has been long accuftomed.

3. If bad habits have, unhappily, been formed, and a man thinks he has ftrength of mind to break through them, he has no other way but refolutely to avoid every affociated circumftance belonging to them,
whatever

whatever can ſo much as lead him to *think* of his former vicious pleaſures; particularly the *company* he has formerly kept, and by whoſe example, inſinuations, and ſolicitations, he has been ſeduced. A man who confides in his fortitude, and wilfully runs into temptation, is almoſt ſure to be overcome. Our only ſafety, in theſe caſes, conſiſts in flying from the danger, through a wiſe diſtruſt of ourſelves.

4. We muſt, alſo, reſolutely do whatever we are convinced is right, whether we can immediately take pleaſure in it or not. Let a man invariably do his duty, and he will, in time, find a real ſatisfaction in it, which will increaſe, as right conduct grows more habitual; till, in time, notwithſtanding the reluctance with which he entered upon a virtuous courſe, he will have the moſt ſincere pleaſure in it, on its own account. He will love virtue for its own ſake, and will not change his courſe of life, even though it ſhould not be the moſt advantageous to him for the preſent.

prefent. If the moft felfifh perfon in the world would make a point of doing generous things, and thus get a cuftom of befriending and relieving others, till he fhould look upon it as his indifpenfable *bufinefs*, and his proper *employment*, he would, at length, find fatisfaction in it, and would act habitually from the pure principles of benevolence.

5. The contemplation of virtuous characters is a great means of infpiring the mind with a love of virtue. If a man attentively confiders the hiftory of a virtuous perfon, he cannot help entering into, and approving his fentiments, and he will intereft himfelf in his fate. In fhort, he will feel himfelf difpofed to act the fame part in the fame circumftances. It is not equally advifable to ftudy the lives, and contemplate the characters of *vicious* perfons, with a view to be deterred from the practice of vice, by means of the horror with which it would infpire us. Becaufe, when the mind is familiarized to any thing,

G the

the horror with which we firſt viewed it, in a great meaſure, ceaſes ; and let a man have been ever ſo wicked, and his ſchemes ever ſo deteſtable, it is hardly poſſible (if his character and hiſtory have been for a long time the principal object of our attention) not to intereſt ourſelves in his affairs, ſo as to be pleaſed with the ſucceſs of his ſchemes and ſtratagems. There will be the more danger of this effect, if ſuch a perſon have any good qualifications to recommend him ; and no man is ſo far abandoned to vice, as to be intirely deſtitute of all amiable and engaging qualities.

Vice joined with wit and humour, or any talent by which a man gives pleaſure, or excites admiration is exceedingly dangerous ; more eſpecially if a perſon of a profligate character be poſſeſſed of any real virtues, particularly ſuch as ſtrike the mind with an idea of *dignity* and *generoſity.* Thus courage, and humanity too often cover and recommend the moſt ſcandalous vices, and even ſuch as really tend to make

men

men cowardly, treacherous, and cruel; and which, at length, extinguish every spark of generosity and goodness in the heart.

6. In order to cultivate the virtues of piety or devotion to the most advantage, it seems necessary that we frequently meditate upon the works, the attributes, and the character of the divine being, and on the benefits which we daily receive from his hands; that we, more especially, reflect upon his universal presence, and providence; till every object, and every occurrence shall introduce the idea of God, as our creator, preserver, benefactor, moral governor, and judge. In this case a regard to him cannot fail habitually to influence our dispositions and conduct, so as to prove the strongest preservative against all vice and wickedness.

7. *Prayer* must be joined to meditation. We must frequently address ourselves to God, expressing our veneration for his

character,

character, our gratitude for his favours
to us, our humiliation for our offences,
our devotednefs to his will, our refignation to his providence, and alfo our *defire*
of any thing that he knows to be really
good for us. This kind of intercourfe
with the deity tends greatly to ftrengthen
every proper difpofition of mind towards
him. Prayer is the univerfal dictate of
nature, not fophifticated by the refine-
ments of philofophy; and, in fact, has
been the practice of all mankind.

Befides, though God be fo great and
good, though he knows all our wants,
and is at all times difpofed to grant us e-
very proper blefling; yet he who made
us, fo as that we cannot help having recourfe to him as our father, benefactor,
and protector, in the fame manner as we
have recourfe to our fuperiors and bene-
factors on earth, will no doubt approve,
encourage, and condefcend to that manner of behaviour and addrefs to him, which
the fame difpofitions and circumftances
necelfarily

neceffarily prompt us to with refpect to one another. We may affure ourfelves, therefore, that the divine being will *realize* our natural conceptions of him, and reward his humble worfhippers. Since we cannot rife to him, and conceive of him in a manner that is ftrictly agreeable to his nature, and fince our intercourfe with him is neceffary to our virtue and happinefs, he will certainly condefcend to us; fo that we may depend upon finding him to be what the beft of his creatures hope, and expect concerning him.

It will not therefore be the fame thing, whether we apply to him for the good things we ftand in need of, or not. Do not the wifeft and beft of parents act in the fame manner towards their children? It has been the fource of great error, and rafh judgment concerning the ways of God, to confine ourfelves to the confideration of what God is *in himfelf*, and not to confider what it even becomes his wifdom and goodnefs, both to reprefent him-

felf,

ſelf, and actually to be, with *reſpect to his*
imperfect creatures.

Beſides, if *good diſpoſitions* be regarded
as the only object and end of prayer, it
ſhould be conſidered, that an addreſs to
God for what we want is a *teſt* of good
diſpoſitions, as well as a *means of improv-*
ing them, ſuppoſing it be known to be the
will of God, that we ſhould pray to him.
But it muſt be acknowledged that, without revelation, or ſome expreſs intimation
of the will of God, in this reſpect, the
reaſonableneſs and obligation of prayer is
not ſo clearly, though ſufficiently evident.

In fact, there are ſimilar reaſons for
aſking favours of God, as for *thanking* him
for the favours we have received; ſince it
may be ſaid, that if we be truly grateful,
it is quite unneceſſary to tell the divine
being that we are ſo; and thus all intercourſe with God by words muſt be cut
off. But certainly there can be no real
impropriety in expreſſing by words what-
                                              ever

ever is the *language of the heart* ; and it, can only be an unreasonable and danger- ous refinement to distinguish, in this case, between love, gratitude, desire, or any other disposition of mind. -

G 3

PART

PART III.

Of the future expectations of mankind.

HAVING endeavoured to inveſti-
gate the rules of human duty, from
the principles of natural reaſon, I ſhall
proceed to aſcertain, from the ſame principles, what we have to expect in conſequence of our obſervance, or neglect of
them.

The natural rewards of virtue, and the
puniſhments of vice, in this life, have
been already mentioned occaſionally. I,
therefore, propoſe, in this ſection, to conſider the evidence with which nature fur-
niſhes us concerning a *future life*, impar-
tially ſtating both its ſtrength and its
weakneſs.

1. The

1. The argument that, in general, has the moſt weight with the wiſe and good, in favour of a future life, is the promiſcuous and unequal diſtribution of good and evil in this world, in a *general*, indeed, but by no means an *exact* proportion to the degrees of moral worth ; which ſeems to be inconſiſtent with the perfect goodneſs and rectitude of God, as our moral governor. If, together with his attributes of infinite wiſdom and power, he be alſo a lover of virtue, may it not be expected, it is ſaid, that he will reward it more completely than is generally done in this world, eſpecially in the caſe of a man ſacrificing his life to his integrity, when he evidently cuts himſelf off from all proſpect of any reward, except in a future ſtate. It is acknowledged, that in this life we find all the perfection we could wiſh, conſidering it as a ſtate of trial and diſcipline in which to *form virtuous characters*, but in order to complete the ſcheme, it ſeems to require another ſtate, to which it may be ſubſervient, and in which the characters

that

that are formed here, may have a fuitable employment and reward.

2. There is in the human faculties a capacity for *endlefs improvement*, in a conftant advance from fenfual to intellectual pleafures, and thefe growing more complex and refined *ad infinitum*, provided it was not checked by that change in our conftitution, which is at prefent produced by our approach to old age. Our *comprehenfion of mind*, likewife, increafes with the experience of every day ; whereby we are capable of enjoying more of the paft and of the future together with the prefent, without limits, and whereby our happinefs is capable of growing continually more ftable and more exalted. In comparifon of what we are evidently capable of, our prefent being is but the infancy of man. Here we acquire no more than the rudiments of knowledge and happinefs. And can it be confiftent with the wifdom of God, to leave his workmanfhip fo unfinifhed, as it muft be, if a final

ftop

ftop be put to all our improvements at death?

It is true, that we have no faculties but what have fome proper exercife in this life, and there is a kind of *redundancy* in all the powers of nature. It is the beft provifion againft a deficiency. Brute creatures too have faculties fimilar to ours, fince they differ from us in *degree* more than in *kind*. But then the difference is fo great, efpecially with refpeft to fome men and fome brutes, and man is fo evidently the moft diftinguifhed of all the creatures of God upon the face of the earth, that there feems to be foundation enough for our expefting a preference in this refpeft. Or, if the brute creation fhould be interefted in a future life, we fhall certainly have more reafon to rejoice in it, than to be offended at it; and many of them feem to have more pain than pleafure in this.

We fee, indeed, that many things never actually arrive at what we call their

perfect.

perfect state. For example, few feeds ever become plants, and few plants live to bear fruit; but ftill *fome* of each fpecies come to maturity, and are whatever their nature is capable of being. Allowing, therefore, that, agreeably to this analogy, very few of mankind fhould arrive at the proper perfection of their natures, we might imagine that, at leaft, *fome* would; and therefore that the wife and the virtuous, if none elfe, might hope to furvive that wreck, that would overwhelm the common mafs of their fpecies.

It muft be acknowledged that, confidering only what we know of the conftitution of the body and the mind of man, we fee no reafon to expect that we fhall furvive death. The faculties and operations of the mind evidently depend upon the ftate of the body, and particularly that of the brain. To all appearance, they grow, decay, and perifh together. But if the goodnefs, the wifdom, and the rectitude of the divine being require it, he he can eafily revive both, or continue the. fame *confcioufnefs* (which is, in fact, *our- felves*) in fome other way,

If we had known nothing of a child but its condition in the womb, we fhould have pronounced, that its fudden tranfition into a ftate fo different from it as that which it comes into after birth, would be certain death to it, though, now that we are acquainted with both the ftates, and can compare them together, we fee that the one is preparatory to the other. Equally unfit are we, in this life, to pro- nounce concerning the real nature of what we call *death*; and when we actually come to live again, we may fee an evident, and even a natural connection betwixt this life and the future, and may then under- ftand the ufe of death, as a paffage from the one to the other; juft as we now fee the neceffity of the birth of a child, in order to its tranfition to our prefent mode of exiftence.

Admitting

Admitting that death is an intire ceſſa-tion of thought, ſimilar to a ſtate of *per-fectly* found ſleep, or a ſtupor, yet, if the purpoſes of God's providence and mo-ral government require it, he can make us to awake from this ſleep at any diſtance of time; and then the interval, let it have been ever ſo long, will appear as nothing to us.

I cannot ſay that I lay much ſtreſs upon the arguments which ſome have drawn ei-ther from the *deſire,* or the *belief* of a future life among mankind; becauſe the former is nothing, in fact, but a deſire of happi-neſs, and ſimilar to other deſires, which, in a thouſand reſpects, we do not ſee to be gratified; and other general opinions may perhaps be mentioned, which, ne-vertheleſs, are not true.

The general belief and expectation of a future life is a conſideration of impor-tance, but only as a proof of an *early tradition,* which was probably denied from
ſome

fome revelation on that fubjeƈt, communicated by God to the firſt parents of mankind.

Upon the whole I cannot help thinking, that there is fomething in the arguments above recited, which fhew that a future life is very agreeable to the appearances of this, though I do not think them fo ſtriking, as to have been fufficient, of themſelves, to have fuggeſted the firſt idea of it. And though, if we had never heard of a future life, we might not have expeƈted it; yet now that we have heard of it, we may be fenſible that we fhould do violence to nature, if we fhould ceaſe to hope for, and believe it.

Admitting that there is another life, taking place either at death, or at fome future period, it muſt be acknowledged, that our condition in it is, at preſent, in a great meaſure unknown to us; but fince the principal arguments in favour of it are drawn from the conſideration of the moral

moral government of God, we may depend upon it, that virtue will find an adequate reward in it, and vice its proper puniſhment. But of what *kind*, it is impoſſible for us to ſay.

We ſeem, however, to have ſufficient reaſon to conclude that, ſince both the happineſs and miſery of a future life will be proportioned to the degrees of virtue and vice in this, they muſt both be *finite*; that is, there muſt be a continuance of virtue, to ſecure a continuance of reward, and a continuance in vice to deſerve a continuance of puniſhment.

Although the goodneſs of God ſhould give a preheminence to *virtue* and the rewards of it, in a future ſtate, yet we do not ſee that even his *juſtice*, in any ſenſe of the word, can require him to do the ſame with reſpect to vice. Indeed, we muſt give up all our ideas of *proportion between crimes and puniſhment*, that is all our ideas of *juſtice* and *equity*, if we ſay that a puniſhment ſtrictly ſpeaking *infinite*, either

either in duration or degree, can be incurred by the fin of a *finite creature*, in a *finite time*, efpecially considering the frailty of human nature, the multiplicity of temptations with which fome poor unhappy wretches are befet, and the great difadvantages they labour under through life.

There is, indeed, a fenfe, and a very alarming one too, in which future punifhments, though not ftrictly fpeaking infinite, may, neverthelefs, be *without end*, and yet be confiftent with the perfect rectitude and goodnefs of God. For the wicked, though confined to a fituation which, after fome time at leaft, may not be abfolutely, and in itfelf, painful, may be for ever excluded from a happier fituation; to which they fee the virtuous advanced. And having this continually in profpect, and knowing that there is an utter impoffibility of their ever regaining the rank they have loft by their vices, they may never ceafe to blame and reproach themfelves for their folly, which

cannot

cannot be recalled, and the effects of which are irreverfible.

If we argue from the analogy of nature, we fhall rather conceive, that, fince pain, and evils of every kind, are falutary in this life, that they will have the fame tendency and operation in a future, and, confequently, that they will be employed to correct, meliorate, and reform thofe who are expofed to them; fo that, after a fufficient time of purification, thofe who are not made virtuous by the fufferings and difcipline of this life, will be recovered to virtue and happinefs by the long continuance of unfpeakably greater fufferings, and of a much *feverer difcipline* in the life to come.

Since, however, the longer we live in this life, the more *fixed* are our habits, and difpofitions of mind, fo that there is an aftonifhing difference between the *flexibility*, as we may call it, of a child, and that of a grown-man, our conftitution after

ter death may be such, as that any change
in the temper of our minds will be brought
about with much more difficulty, so that
a space of time almost incredible to us at
present, may be neceſſary, in order that
the sufferings of a future life may have
their proper effect, in reforming a perſon
who dies a ſlave to vicious habits.

The motives to virtue by no means loſe
any of their real force from the conſideration of the *non eternity* of *future puniſhments,* eſpecially upon the ſuppoſition that
they will be very intenſe, and laſting,
though not abſolutely *without end.* For,
in the firſt place, what is loſt with reſpect
to the motive of *terror* and aſtoniſhment,
is gained by that of *love,* and the perſuaſion of the greater regard, in the divine
being, both to juſtice and mercy, in *not
retaining anger for ever,* on account of the
finite offences of his imperfect creatures.
Secondly, If the mind of any man be ſo
hardened, that he will not be influenced
by the expectation of a very long continu-

tinuance of puniſhment, a thouſand
years for inſtance, he will not, in fact,
be influenced by the expectation of any
ſuffering at all, even that of eternal
and infinite ſuffering. For, in reality,
if the fear of the former do not affect him,
and ſtop his career of vice, it muſt be
owning to his not allowing himſelf time
to think and reflect upon the ſubject.
For no man who really *thinks* and *believes*,
can be guilty of ſuch extreme folly, as to
purchaſe a momentary gratification at ſo
diſproportioned a price; and if a man do
not think about the matter, but will follow his appetites and paſſions without any
reflection, all difference, in the inten-
ſity or duration of puniſhment, is wholly
loſt upon him.

In fact, we ſee that the bulk of profeſ-
ſing chriſtians, who, if they were aſked,
would acknowledge their belief of the
eternity of hell torments, are by no means
effectually deterred from vice by their belief of it. Rather, the vaſtneſs of the
thing creates a kind of *ſecret incredulity.*
They

They have a notion that the thing may not, in reality, take place; and, thinking of no medium, they fecretly flatter themfelves with the hope of meeting with no punifhment at all, and confequently indulge the vain hope of going to heaven, with a ftate of mind exceedingly unfit for it, rather than fuffer a punifhment fo vaftly difproportioned to the degree of their guilt. Whereas, if they had been taught to expect only a *juft* and *adequate* punifhment, for all their offences here; and efpecially fuch as was neceffary to their purification and happinefs, their minds might have acquiefed in it, they might have believed it firmly and practically, and fuch a belief might really have influenced their conduct.

-But laftly, it is perhaps more agreeable to the analogy of nature and (this guide only I am now following) to expect, that, as the greater part of natural productions never arrive at their proper maturity, but perifh long before they have

attained

attained to it, fo the bulk of mankind, who never attain to any high degrees of wifdom or virtue, fhould finally perifh alfo, and be entirely blotted out of the creation, as unworthy to continue in it; while the few who are wife and virtuous, like full ripe fruits, are referved for future ufe. And there is fomething fo dreadful in the idea of *annihilation*, as will, perhaps, affect the mind of fome perfons more than the fear of future torments, with continuance of life, and confequently with fecret hope.

These fpeculations, it muft be owned, are, in a great meafure, random and vague, but they are the beft, as it appears to me, that we can form to ourfelves by the light of nature. What revelation teaches us concerning fo difficult but important a fubject, we fhall fee in its proper place.

Such are the conclufions which nature teaches or rather which fhe *afferts to* concerning the nature, and perfections of
'God,

God, the rule of human duty, and the future expectations of mankind. I fay *affents to,* becaufe, if we examine the actual ftate of this kind of knowledge, in any part of the world, not enlightened by revelation, we fhall find their ideas of God, of virtue, and of a future ftate, to have been very lame and imperfect, as will be fhewn more particularly when we confider, in the next part of this courfe, the *want* and the *evidence* of D I V I N E REVELATION.

F I N I S.

BOOKS written
By JOSEPH PRIESTLEY, L. L. D. F. R. S.
And Sold by
J. JOHNSON, Bookseller, at No. 72, in St.
Paul's Church-Yard, London.

AN Essay on the first Principles of Government,
and on the Nature of Political, Civil, and
Religious Liberty, including Remarks on Dr Brown's
Code of Education, and on Dr. Balguy's Sermon on
Church Authority, the Second Edition, corrected
and enlarged, Price 5s.

2. A Free Address to Protestant Dissenters, on the
Subject of the Lord's Supper, the Second Edit. 1s.

3. A Catechism for Children and Young Persons, 6d.

4. A Scripture Catechism, consisting of a set of
questions only, with references to the Scriptures
instead of *answers*.

5. A Serious Address to Masters of Families,
with Forms of Family Prayer, 9d.

6. A View of the Principles and Conduct of the
Protestant Dissenters, with Respect to the Civil and
Ecclesiastical Constitution of England, the Second
Edition, 1s. 6d.

7. A Free Address to Protestant Dissenters on the
Subject of Church-Discipline, 2s. 6d.

- *Also published,* In Numbers,
(Under the Direction of Dr. PRIESTLEY.)
The THEOLOGICAL REPOSITORY; consist-
ing of Original Essays, Hints, Queries, &c. calculated to promote Religious Knowledge.
N. B. Two Volumes of this work, price 6s. each,
are already completed.

ALSO, Sold by Mr. JOHNSON,
A Free Address to Protestant Dissenters as
such, by a Dissenter, the Second Edition, Price 1s.

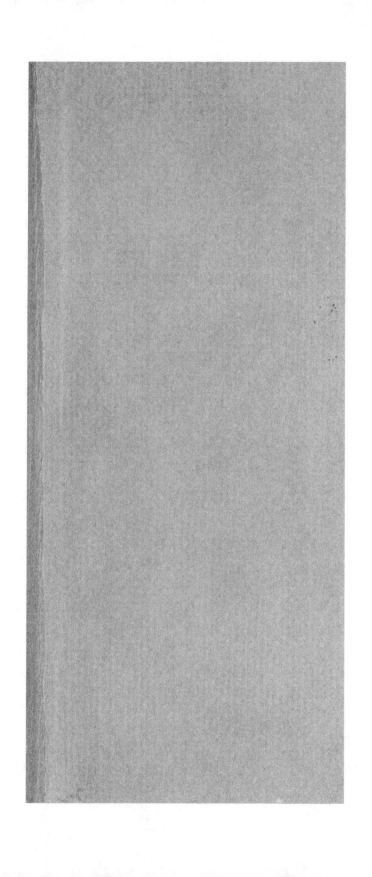

CPSIA information can be obtained
at www.ICGtesting.com
Printed in the USA
LVHW030427220322
714056LV00004B/105